Table of Contents

Renal

Multisystem

Behavioral/Psychosocial

Professional Care and Ethical Practice

Cardiovascular

The heart is a complex organ that contains three layers: the epicardium, the myocardium, and the endocardium. The pericardium is the sac that surrounds the heart and the roots of several vessels. The heart has four hollow chambers: the right atria, left atria, right ventricle, and left ventricle. Blood flows from chamber to chamber through valves. The vascular system (circulatory system) involves arterial and venous blood flow. Arteries deliver blood to the heart, whereas venous vessels take blood to the organs and body structures.

Anatomy and Physiology

Terms

- Aneurysm - Abnormal dilation of artery
- Angina - Chest pain described as spasmodic and choking
- Angiography - Diagnostic test on the blood vessels
- Angioplasty - Procedure used to dilate a vessel opening
- Bundle of His - Cardiac fibers that allow heart rhythm
- Circumflex - A coronary artery that encircles the heart
- Edema - Swelling due to fluid collection in the tissue
- Electrophysiology - The study of the heart's electrical system
- Embolectomy - Removal of an embolism or blockage from a vessel.
- Epicardial - Over the heart.
- Fistula - Opening from one area to the other or to the outside of the body
- Hemolysis - RBC breakdown
- Intracardiac - Inside the heart
- Thoracostomy - Incisions made into the chest wall to insert a chest tube
- Transvenous - Through a vein

CIRCULATION OF BLOOD THROUGH THE HEART

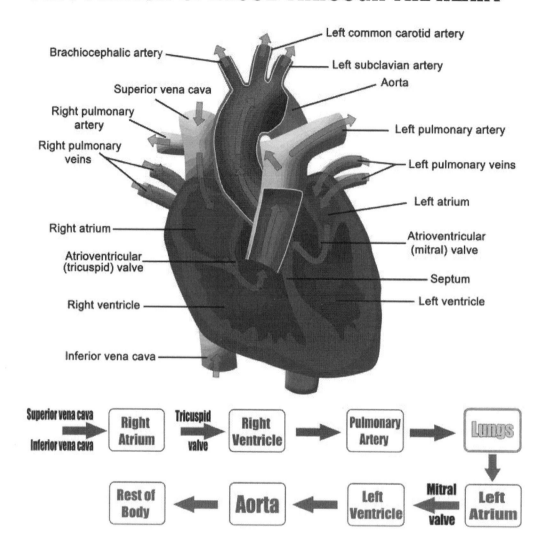

Heart

The heart is a muscular organ that has two pumps, the left and right ventricles. The left ventricle receives oxygenated blood from the lungs and sends it throughout the body. The right pump receives oxygen-poor blood, and sends it to the lungs.

Blood

- Function - To maintain a constant environment, carry oxygen and nutrients to cells, delivery waste and carbon dioxide to organs, and transport hormones from the endocrine system.

- Liquid - Plasma is extracellular with 91% water.

- Cellular - Contains leukocytes (white blood cells WBCs), erythrocytes (red blood cells or RBCs), and thrombocytes (platelets).

Vessels

- Function - To transport blood and carry away cellular waste and carbon dioxide.

- Arteries - Lead away from the heart and branch into arterioles.

- Veins - Lead to the heart and branch into venules.

- Capillaries - Connect between arterioles and venules

Heart Muscle Layers

- Endocardium - Smooth lining inside the heart.

- Myocardium - Thick muscular heart wall.

- Epicardium - Outer layer of the heart and inner layer of pericardium.

- Pericardium - Fibrous sac around the heart.

Heart Chambers and Valves

- Atria - The two upper heart chambers. The atria pumps blood into the ventricles right before they contract, which is called an "atrial kick."

- Ventricles - The lower heart chambers that receive blood from the atria and send it throughout the body during ventricular contraction. Ventricular contraction generates a palpable pulse.

- Heart valves - One-way valves between the atria and ventricles, which allow blood to move in a downward direction into the ventricles during atrial contraction.

Conduction System

The heart has a conduction (electrical) system, which generates electrical impulses and stimulates heart muscle contraction. The primary area is the sinoatrial (SA) node, which generates anywhere from 60 to 100 impulses per minute in the adult. The backup pacemaker is the atrioventricular (AV) junction, which generates electrical impulses at around 40 to 60 per minute. The bundle of His is a pacemaker that can generate around 20 to 40 impulses per minute.

Cardiac Contraction

- Myocardial contractility - The ability of the heart to contract, which requires adequate blood volume and muscle strength.

- Preload - The pre-contraction pressure based on the amount of blood that flows back to the heart. An increased preload leads to increased ventricular stretching and increased contractility.

- Afterload - The resistance which the heart must overcome during contraction of the ventricles. If there is an increase in afterload, there is decreased cardiac output.

Blood Flow

Blood flows through the cardiovascular system in a complex method. Oxygen-rich blood leaves the heart via the aorta, which branches off into arteries, then arterioles, and then capillaries. The capillaries feed into the venules, to the veins, and then into the superior or inferior vena cava.

Arteries carry blood away from the heart and veins carry blood to the heart. The pulmonary artery carries deoxygenated blood, where the pulmonary vein carries oxygen-rich blood.

Blood Flow in Human Circulatory System

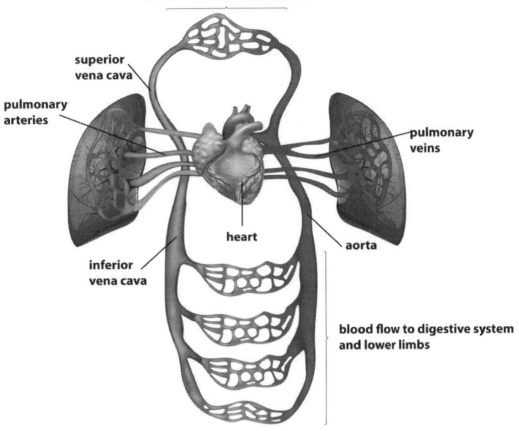

The Path of Blood Flow

- The vena cava returns blood to the right atrium.

- The right atrium pumps blood into the right ventricle.

- The right ventricle pumps oxygen-poor blood to the pulmonary arteries and then to the lungs.

- Carbon dioxide and oxygen exchange occurs between the alveoli and capillaries.

- The lungs send oxygen-rich blood to the heart via the pulmonary veins.

- Blood enters the left atrium which pumps blood to the left ventricle.

- From the left ventricle, the blood enters the aorta for circulation throughout the body.

Systemic Vascular Resistance (SVR)

Systemic vascular resistance (SVR) is a resistance to blood flow in the body, but this excludes the pulmonary system. SVR is related to the blood vessel size:

- Constriction - This is reduced size, which increases SVR and blood pressure

- Dilation - This is increased size, which lowers SVR and blood pressure

Components of the Blood

- Plasma - Liquid that is mostly water

- Platelets - Necessary for clot formation to stop bleeding

- Red blood cells (RBCs) - Also called erythrocytes, these cells carry oxygen

- White blood cells (WBCs) - Also called leukocytes, these cells fight infection

Blood Pressure

Blood pressure (BP) is a measurement of pressure exerted against the artery walls. The systolic pressure is when the blood pressure exerts during contraction of the left ventricle, and diastolic pressure is the pressure between contractions.

Blood Perfusion

Blood perfusion is the flow of blood through the body. When there is adequate perfusion, the organs and tissues receive oxygen-rich blood. However, with inadequate perfusion, also called shock, the blood flow is compromised.

Pharmacology

One of the main roles of the critical care nurse is the administration and titration of medications. Various cardiovascular drugs are used for homeostasis. The main classes of drugs are preload reduction agents, afterload reduction agents, vasopressor agents, inotropic agents, antiarrhythmic agents, antianginals, lipid-lowering agents, antihypertensives, calcium channel blockers, thrombolytics, antiplatelet agents, and anticoagulants.

Preload Reduction Agents

These are used to reduce preload in the critically ill patient. Preload reduction agents work by causing venous dilation, which then decreases the filling pressure of the heart. The most common type of this agent is diuretics.

These include:

- Loop diuretics – Furosemide and ethacrynic acid which acts on the loop of Henle.

- Osmotic diuretics – Mannitol

- Thiazides – Hydrochlorothiazide that inhibits sodium reabsorption.

- Potassium-sparing diuretics – Amiloride hydrochloride and spironolactone which promote sodium secretion and potassium reabsorption.

- Vasodilators – Coronary vasodilators, such as morphine and nitrates, are used to treat myocardial pain. Nitroprusside and nitroglycerin are direct smooth muscle relaxants which cause vasodilation. Nitroprusside is used to reduce acute hypertension and for afterload reduction in patients with heart failure. Nitroglycerin reduces filling pressure and dilates the coronary arteries.

- Beta blockers – These drugs decrease heart rate and contractility and increase diastolic filling pressure. Atenolol, esmolol, metoprolol, and labetalol are commonly used beta blockers. To prevent rebound effects, such as palpitations, hypertension, and unstable angina, care must be taken to not withdraw these medications too rapidly.

Afterload Reduction Agents

- Angiotensin-converting enzyme inhibitors (ACEIs) – These agents reduce afterload and cause vasodilation, which in turn decreases the left ventricle's workload. They also block the conversion of angiotensin I to angiotensin II. Hypotension is a complication of ACEIs, and examples include enalapril and captopril.

- Angiotensin II receptor blockers (ARBs) – These drugs work much like ACEIs. They block the effects of angiotensin II (chemical that contracts vessels), and dilate vessels to decrease blood pressure. Irbesartan, losartan, and valsartan are ARBs that work well for patient s with heart failure, hypertension, and those who cannot take ACEIs.

- Hydralazine – This drug is a potent arterial smooth muscle dilator that is given IV. A typical dose is slow push at 5 to 10 mg every 4 to 6 hours. One side effect of hydralazine is reflex tachycardia, which can be given intermittently.

Vasopressor Agents

Vasopressors are sympathomimetic drugs that control peripheral vasoconstriction and increase afterload and systemic vascular resistance. Three common vasopressors are norepinephrine, neosynephrine and vasopressin. Risks must be evaluated when considering the use of these drugs.

Inotropic Agents

Inotropic drugs improve cardiac contractility and improve cardiac output:

- Milirinone – This medication relaxes the smooth muscle of vessels and increases myocardial contractility. The loading dose is 50 mcg/kg over 10 minutes followed by IV infusion of 0.375 to 0.75 mcg/kg/minute.

- Digoxin – This drug stimulates adrenergic receptors and the sympathetic nervous system.

- Dobutamine – This agent has alpha- and beta-adrenergic effects to increase blood flow to the kidneys and mesentery through vasodilation. A moderate dose is 2 to 10 mcg/kg/minute, which will increase blood pressure, heart rate and tissue perfusion.

Anti-Arrhythmic Agents

Anti-arrhythmic agents are classified as Class I through IV. The class of drug depends on the drug's action. These are:

- Class 1A – Quinidine and procainamide (sodium channel blockers)

- Class IB – Lidocaine (sodium channel blocker)

- Class II – Metoprolol and propranolol (beta blockers)

- Class III – Amiodarone (slow depolarization)

- Class IV – Diltiazem and verapamil (calcium channel blockers)

- Unclassified – Adenosine and magnesium

Pathophysiology

Acute Coronary Syndromes

Acute coronary syndrome (ACS) is a term used to describe a spectrum of clinical conditions, which include ST-segment elevation myocardial infarction (STEMI), non-ST-segment elevation myocardial infarction (NSTEMI), and unstable angina (UA). This syndrome is usually associated with rupture of an atherosclerotic plaque and thrombosis of an artery.

Causes of ACS

The primary cause of ACS is atherosclerosis. Many cases of ACS occur due to disruption of an atherosclerotic lesion that is vulnerable to rupture. The plaque consists of a large lipid pool, many inflammatory cells, and a fibrous cap. ACS occurs when there is high-grade coronary obstruction, which often results from emotional stress, dehydration, infection, hypotension, thyrotoxicosis, or surgery. The main trigger for coronary thrombosis is plaque rupture, which occurs due to dissolution of the fibrous cap and release of the activated inflammatory cells. After this event, platelet activation, platelet aggregation, coagulation pathway activation, and vasoconstriction occur.

STAGES OF ATHEROSCLEROSIS

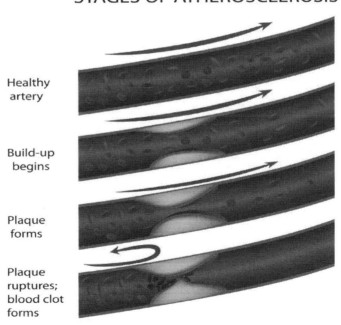

Healthy artery

Build-up begins

Plaque forms

Plaque ruptures; blood clot forms

Signs and Symptoms

- Chest Pain – Typical described as pressure, burning, and/or squeezing across the mid-sternal region and radiating to the shoulder, neck, jaw, back, either arm, and/or upper abdomen

- Palpitations – Perception of rapid heart rate

- Diaphoresis – Associated with sympathetic discharge

- Exertional dyspnea – May or may not resolve with rest

- Nausea – Related to vagal stimulation

- Exercise Intolerance – A decrease in exercise tolerance

Physical Findings

- Hypertension – Can precipitate angina and reflect elevated catecholamine levels.

- Hypotension – Can indicate ventricular dysfunction due to myocardial ischemia, acute valvular dysfunction, or myocardial infarction (MI).

- Jugular vein distension (JVD)

- Systolic murmur, third heart sound (S3), and/or fourth heart sound (S4)

- Pulmonary edema and rales

- Diaphoresis

Diagnosis

- ECG – The most important diagnostic test for angina in the emergency setting is electrocardiogram (ECG). In the unit setting, telemetry monitoring often is involved with diagnosis. ECG changes seen during an episode of angina include:
  - ST depressions – May be down sloping, horizontal, or junctional.
  - Transient ST-segment elevations
  - T wave changes – Such as normalizations, inversions, or hyper-acute changes.

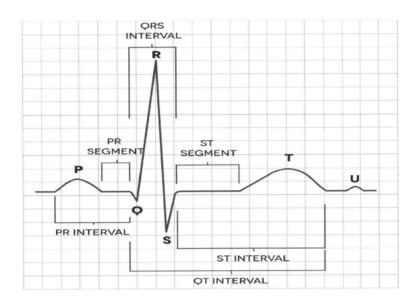

- Laboratory Tests – the laboratory tests that are used to diagnose ACS include:
    - Creatine kinase isoenzyme MB (CK-MB) levels
    - Myoglobin levels
    - Cardiac troponin levels
    - Complete blood count
    - Basic metabolic panel

- Imaging Tests – these include:
    - Chest x-ray
    - Myocardial perfusion imaging
    - Computed tomography (CT)
    - Cardiac angiography

Treatment and Management

The initial treatment for the patient with ACS involves:

- Relieving the chest pain

- Stabilizing the patient

- Providing antithrombotic therapy

Pharmacologic Therapy

- Aspirin

- Nitrates

- Beta blockers

- Clopidogrel

- Prasugrel

- Ticagrelor

- Glycoprotein IIb/IIIa receptor antagonists (epitafibatide, abciximab, tirofiban)

- Unfractionated heparin (UFH)

- Factor Xa inhibitors

- Low-molecular-weight heparin (LMWH)

Percutaneous Coronary Intervention

The preferred treatment for ST-elevation MI is percutaneous coronary intervention (PCI). Patients with MI or STEMI with a new left bundle branch block need to have PCI within 90 minutes of the event. PCI is also necessary for those patients with NSTEMI and high-risk factors, such as recurrent angina, elevated cardiac enzymes, ST-segment depression, sustained ventricular tachycardia, hemodynamic instability, and history of PCI or bypass surgery.

PCI involves diagnostic angiography along with angioplasty and stenting. This is done to restore coronary blood flow. Many studies show that PCI has an advantage over fibrinolysis regarding bleeding rates, short-term mortality, and reinfarction.

Patient Education

- Risk factors – The CCRN should educate the patient on the risk factors for ACS, as well as the signs and symptoms.

- Smoking cessation – The patient should be educated on the dangers of cigarette smoking and needs to be encouraged to stop.

- Dietary measures – Diet contributes to the development of coronary artery disease (CAD), so the patient should be instructed on the American Heart Association's (AHA) low-fat, low-cholesterol diet.

Acute Myocardial Infarction/Ischemia

Patients who experience an acute myocardial infarction (AMI) complain of gradual or sudden onset of anterior chest pain/discomfort, which is usually described as heaviness or pressure. AMI falls in the spectrum of ACSs, and occurs when there is persistent elevation of the ST-segment from total occlusion of a coronary artery. This leads to cardiac tissue necrosis and ischemia (STEMI). When there is no ST-segment elevation, it is referred to as NSTEMI or UA.

Epidemiology

It is estimated that as many as 500,000 episodes of AMI occur in the U.S. each year, affecting around 600 in 6 in every 1,000 men and 2 in every 1,000 women. The World Health Organization (WHO) reported that around 17 million individuals died from CAD in 2004, which represented 30 percent of global deaths.

Causes of AMI

The primary cause of AMI is the rupture of high-risk plaque in the coronary arteries. Approximately 90 percent of STEMI patients and around 50 percent of NSTEMI and UA patients have thrombus formation in their coronary arteries. There are many well-established risk factors for atherosclerosis, such as male gender, age, diabetes, smoking, dyslipidemia, hypertension, and family history.

- Age – People over the age of 45 years have an eight times greater chance of having AMI, and the risk for mortality after an AMI is higher for older persons.

- Diabetes – People with diabetes have an increased risk of AMI because elevated glucose levels will increase the rate of atherosclerotic progression, and diabetes affects the lipid profile.

- Smoking – Cigarette smoking increases AMI risk, and this risk is proportional to the number of cigarettes smoked per day.

- Dyslipidemia – Elevated low-density lipoprotein (LDL) cholesterol and triglyceride levels increase AMI risk.

- Hypertension – Elevated blood pressure in both systolic and diastolic hypertension increases AMI risk. The control of blood pressure has been shown to significantly reduce the risk of MI.

- Family history – People with a first-degree relative with AMI have an increased risk.

Why AMI Occurs

AMI occurs when there is a diminished blood supply to the heart muscle, and this overwhelms the muscle cellular repair mechanisms and the maintenance of homeostasis. Ischemia results in irreversible myocardial cell damage or death, and there is a decreased amount of oxygen and blood nutrients to the myocardium and coronary circulation. The interruption of blood flow occurs when a thrombus or unstable atherosclerotic plaque occludes the coronary vessel.

The development of a plaque occurs over several years or decades. When there is structural stability loss of a plaque, it can break loose from the vessel wall. With disruption of the endothelial surface, a thrombus forms via platelet activation and coagulation. When the thrombus is large enough to block blood flow, an AMI occurs.

Classification and Severity of AMI

Myocardial infarction is classified on the basis of morphologic, anatomic, and diagnostic clinical information. Based on diagnostic findings on ECG, there are two types of MI: STEMI and NSTEMI. The two types of MI are transmural and non-transmural.

- Transmural – This type of MI is associated with ischemic necrosis of the full thickness of a muscle part, and the necrosis affects the endocardium, myocardium, and epicardium.

- Non-transmural – This type of MI is associated with ischemic necrosis that does not extend through the full thickness of the myocardial wall.

Three factors that determine the severity of an MI are:

- The length of time of the occlusion – The longer the period of occlusion, the greater the chances of myocardial cell and tissue death.

- The level of the occlusion – The more proximal the occlusion, the more extensive the tissue necrosis.

- The presence or absence of collateral circulation.

Signs and Symptoms of AMI

The signs and symptoms of AMI vary from patient to patient. Many diabetic individuals experience asymptomatic MI. However, the characteristic signs and symptoms include:

- Chest pain described as squeezing, fullness, and/or pressure in the mid-thoracic region.

- Pain that radiates to the shoulder, arm, back, jaw, and/or neck.

- Dyspnea

- Epigastric discomfort, which is often accompanied by nausea and/or vomiting.

- Diaphoresis

- Syncope or near syncope

- Altered cognitive functioning

Diagnosis

- ECG – Electrocardiography is the first test done to diagnose AMI

- Laboratory Tests – These include creatine kinase, troponin I and T, and myoglobin

- Echocardiogram – Often called an echo, this test is done to compare areas of the left ventricle functioning. It is also used to find which portion of the heart is damaged by the AMI.

Treatment and Management

The goals of treatment for AMI are to salvage the function of the myocardium and restore normal coronary blood flow. With acute STEMI, "time is muscle," so early treatment is vital.

- Antiplatelet Agents – Aspirin is given in a dose of 325 mg when there are signs and symptoms of AMI. This drug interferes with the function of cyclooxygenase and prevents the formation of a thromboxane A2, and prevents platelet aggregation and adhesion. Several studies recommend the use of clopidogrel along with aspirin.

- Oxygen – Supplemental oxygen is given to assure that erythrocytes are saturated to their maximum carrying capacity.

- Nitrates – Nitrates are given for vasodilation of coronary arteries, but are contraindicated when a patient has severe pump dysfunction or residual ischemia.

- Morphine – This opiate is the drug of choice for pain control.

- Beta Blocker – A beta blocker, such as atenolol, is given within 12 hours of AMI symptoms to decrease the incidence of ventricular arrhythmias, reinfarction, recurrent ischemia, and infarct size.

- Unfractionated Heparin – UFN is used until the ruptured plaque is resolved or healed. This medication prevents thrombus formation and is given 48 hours post AMI.

- Low-molecular-weight Heparin – LMWH is used in AMI patients who are not treated with fibrinolytic therapy.

- Fibrinolytics – These agents are used for restoration of coronary blood flow in AMI patients who present with STEMI, and it is given within 12 hours of symptom onset.

- Angiotensin-converting Enzyme Inhibitors and Angiotensin Receptor Blockers – ACE inhibitors are used for AMI patients with STEMI who have heart failure, hypertension, diabetes, or an ejection fraction of less than 40 percent. ARBS can be used for patients who are sensitive or allergic to ACE inhibitors.

- Glycoprotein IIb/IIIa Antagonists – These medications work by inhibiting platelet aggregation.

- Percutaneous Coronary Intervention – This is used for patients with AMI to restore coronary blood flow.

- Surgical Revascularization – This is accomplished through emergent or urgent coronary artery bypass grafting (CABG), and is warranted for patients of failed PCI.

- Implantable Cardiac Defibrillators – Automatic defibrillators are used to decrease mortality post-AMI for patients with depressed ejection fractions.

Medication Dosing for ACS and AMI Patients

Beta Blocker Therapy

Drug	Dosing
Carvedilol	6.25 mg bid titrated to 25 mg bid
Metoprolol	15 mg IV x 1, then 200 mg/day PO
Atenolol	5-10 mg IV x 1, then 100 mg/day PO

Unfractionated Heparin

Loading Dose	60 U/kg IV bolus
Maintenance Dose	12 U/kg/hr IV
Titration Goal	PTT 50-70 sec

Low-Molecular-Weight Heparin

Drug	After SC Dosing	ACS Dosing	Indications
Enoxaparin	4.5 hr	100 U/kg or 1 mg/kg	Complications of NSTEMI and UA
Dalteparin	3-5 hr	120 U/dg SC bid	Prevention of complications in NSTEMI and UA

ACE Inhibitors

Drug	Dose
Captopril	6.25 mg tid titrated to 50 mg tid
Lisinopril	5 mg/day titrated to 10 mg/day
Ramipril	1.25 mg bid titrated to 5 mg bid

Acute Peripheral Vascular Insufficiency

Peripheral Arterial Occlusive Disease

Peripheral arterial occlusive disease (PAOD) is caused by atherosclerosis, and it leads to claudication, which is reproducible ischemic muscle pain. This pain occurs during activity and is relieved with rest, and it occurs due to inadequate blood perfusion to the tissues.

Diagnosis of PAOD

The diagnosis of PAOD is made by a complete lower extremity evaluation, which includes measurement of segmental pressures and pulse examination. Testing involves:

- Doppler – Used to assess circulation.
- Ankle-brachial index (ABI) – Calculated as the ratio of systolic blood pressure at the ankle compared to the arm (normal range is 0.0 to 1.1 and PAOD is < 0.9).
- Angiography – Arterial imaging study.

28

- Magnetic resonance angiography (MRA) – Test used to assess both large and small vessels.

- Duplex ultrasonography – Noninvasive test that evaluates vascular status.

Treatment and Management of PAOD

The treatment of PAOD is usually medical, but surgery is required for severe cases. Surgical measures for the treatment of PAOD include endovascular stenting, balloons, atherectomy devices and open bypass surgery. Conservative medical measures include:

- Smoking cessation

- Exercise program

- Control of lipid profile, hypertension, and glucose levels

- Antiplatelet therapy

Mortality and Morbidity

The worst consequence of PAOD is ischemia that leads to amputation of a limb. This depends on the severity of cardiovascular risk factors. Predicted mortality rates for patients with claudication at 5, 10, and 15 years are 30 percent, 50 percent, and 70 percent, respectively.

Carotid Artery Stenosis

Carotid artery stenosis is narrowing of a carotid artery. The carotid arteries carry oxygen-rich blood to the brain from the heart, and stenosis occurs when there is buildup of atherosclerotic plaque in the artery wall. Older patients are more likely to have carotid stenosis, with men more at risk than women. Also, a person who has an elevated lipid profile, hypertension, and a cigarette habit is eight times more likely to develop carotid artery stenosis. Of the 500,000 strokes that occur in the U.S. each year, carotid stenosis causes around 25 percent of them.

Trans-Atlantic Inter-Society Consensus II (TASC II) Guidelines

The Trans-Atlantic Inter-Society Consensus II established guidelines for treatment of peripheral vascular disease. The TASC II is based on lesion characteristics. For aorto-iliac lesions:

- TASC A – Unilateral or bilateral stenosis of the common iliac artery (CIA) and unilateral or bilateral single short stenosis of the external iliac artery (EIA).

- TASC B – Unilateral CIA occlusion, single or multiple stenosis of 3-10 cm of the EIA but not the femoral artery, and unilateral EIA occlusion.

- TASC C – Infra-renal aortic occlusion, disease of the aorta and both iliac arteries, multiple stenosis of EIA, CIA, and femoral arteries, and calcified EIA occlusion.

- TASC D – Infra-renal aortic occlusion, multiple stenosis of the EIA, CIA, and femoral arteries, disease of the aorta and both iliac arteries, unilateral occlusion of both CIA and EIA, iliac stenosis along with an abdominal aortic aneurysm (AAA), and bilateral EIA occlusion.

Stroke Risk

The three ways carotid stenosis increases the risk of stroke are:

- Plaque deposits deform the artery wall and cause blood clots to form.

- Plaque deposits enlarge and narrow the artery.

- Plaque deposits rupture, break free, and travel to a small artery in the brain.

Signs and Symptoms of Carotid Artery Stenosis

The symptoms of carotid stenosis usually appear as a TIA, but many patients have no symptoms. Typical TIA and/or stroke symptoms include:

- Visual changes

- Drooping face

- Weakness or numbness of an arm and/or leg

Diagnosis of Carotid Artery Stenosis

To diagnose carotid stenosis, several laboratory and diagnostic tests are done. These include:

- Lipid profile

- Complete blood count

- Electrolytes

- Creatine and blood urea nitrogen

- Prothrombin time and activated partial thromboplastin time

- Carotid duplex ultrasonography

- Electrocardiogram

- Cranial CT and/or magnetic resonance imaging (MRI)

Treatment and Management

Atherosclerosis and stenosis of the carotid artery treatment depends on the degree and severity of the disease. Medications used include antiplatelet agents (aspirin, clopidogrel, and ticlopidine) and anticoagulants (warfarin). Endovascular surgical procedures, such as stenting, angioplasty, and endarterectomy are done for some patients.

Endarterectomy

Atherosclerosis of the carotid artery is caused by stenosis, thrombosis, and embolization. It is also associated with transient ischemic attacks (TIAs), amaurosis fugax (transient visual loss), cerebral infarction, and stroke. When a patient has carotid artery disease, it is treated with carotid endarterectomy. This procedure is indicated for symptomatic patients with greater than 70 percent stenosis, and asymptomatic patients with greater than 60 percent stenosis. A carotid endarterectomy is contraindicated for patients with severe neurological deficit following a cerebral infarction or an occluded carotid artery.

Carotid Angioplasty/Stenting

Carotid angioplasty/stenting is done by a minimally invasive procedure where the plaque is compressed to widen the artery lumen. This is done during an angiogram with a flexible catheter that is inserted in the femoral artery. This procedure is reserved for patients with moderate to high-grade stenosis greater than 70 percent, or for patients who have multiple risk factors.

Carotid Artery Bypass

The carotid artery bypass is a procedure that is done to redirect the blood flow around the stenosed region of the artery. The surgeon will use an artery or vein from the patient's body to serve as the graft, such as the saphenous vein of the leg or one of the radial arteries. This surgery is only done when there is 100 percent blockage of the carotid artery.

Peripheral Stents

Peripheral arterial occlusive lesions are usually managed with peripheral stenting. For many patients, endoluminal catheter-based technique is the treatment of choice. Peripheral stenting involves the placement of a metal stent across the stenosed vessel. Indications for peripheral stents in the extremities include:

- Severe and debilitating intermittent claudication
- Ischemia with pain during rest
- Non-healing ischemic ulcers of the lower extremity
- Subclavian steal syndrome (syncope or dizziness with arm use)
- Subclavian stenosis

Fem-Pop Bypass

Femoral popliteal (fem-pop) bypass surgery is a procedure that is used to treat severe femoral artery blockage caused by plaque. The femoral and popliteal arteries of the legs supply oxygen-rich blood to the lower extremities, and are often referred to as the peripheral arteries. When peripheral arterial disease occurs, this procedure is necessary to alleviate symptoms and prevent complications.

The fem-pop bypass procedure is done through a small incision of the upper leg to allow for direct visualization of the femoral artery. The blocked portion of the artery is bypassed using a piece of another vessel (graft), which is taken from another vein of the leg. The blood is rerouted around the blockage using the graft.

Percutaneous Transluminal Angioplasty (PTA)

Percutaneous transluminal angioplasty (PTA) of the femoral arteries is a procedure where arterial blood flow is restored to the lower leg by way of a special technique. A catheter is inserted into the artery through a small incision, and when the balloon is inflated, the plaque is compressed to open the narrow portion. A stent (tiny metal coil) can be used to keep the area open.

Complications of Arterial Surgery

- Myocardial infarction
- Cardiac arrhythmias
- Wound infection
- Hemorrhage
- Leg edema
- Thrombosis
- Pulmonary edema
- Restenosis
- Graft occlusion
- Nerve injury

Acute Pulmonary Edema

Also called cardiogenic pulmonary edema (CPE), acute pulmonary edema occurs from increased capillary hydrostatic pressure that is due to elevated pulmonary venous pressure. This causes accumulation of low-protein fluid in the lung interstitium and alveoli. The main complications of CPE are respiratory failure and sudden cardiac death due to cardiac arrhythmia.

Causes of CPE

- Increased pulmonary capillary pressure

- Increased negative interstitial pressure

- Decreased plasma oncotic pressure

- Lymphatic obstruction

- Alveolar-capillary barrier damage

- Excessive intravascular volume administration

- Mitral stenosis

- Left ventricular heart failure

Stages of CPE

- Stage 1 – In this stage, elevated left atrial pressure causes distention and dilation of small pulmonary vessels.

- Stage 2 – During stage 2, fluid in the lung interstitium shifts from the pulmonary capillaries, and there is fluid collection in the interstitial compartment, which is the large vessel tissue. This leads to mild hypoxemia, tachypnea, and increased respiratory and heart rates.

- Stage 3 – With the final stage, fluid filtration continues to increase and fluid accumulates in interstitial space. As the fluid crosses the alveolar epithelium into the alveoli, there is poor gas exchange, and reduction of respiratory volume. This leads to worsening of hypoxemia.

Cardiac Conditions associated with CPE

- LV systolic dysfunction – Chronic LV failure is exacerbated by severe anemia, acute MI, excessive sodium intake, noncompliance with medications, thyrotoxicosis, sepsis, myocarditis, myocardial toxins, aortic stenosis, mitral regurgitation, and aortic regurgitation

- LV diastolic dysfunction – LV diastolic dysfunction is caused by ischemia and infarction, as well as pericarditis and tamponade

- Dysrhythmias – Atrial fibrillation and ventricular tachycardia can cause CPE

- LV hypertrophy and cardiomyopathies – These conditions can result in increased LV stiffness and elevated end-diastolic pressure

- Aortic valve stenosis – LV outflow obstruction can cause CPE

Treatment and Management

The initial treatment of CPE involves the ABCs of resuscitation: airway, breathing, and circulation. Some of the therapies used include:

- Supplemental oxygen – Oxygen is administered to patients to keep O2 saturation above 90 percent. For some patients, it may be necessary to use noninvasive pressure support ventilation, such as bi-level positive airway pressure (BiPAP) and continuous positive airway pressure (CPAP), or mechanical ventilation.

- Ultrafiltration – This procedure involves the removal of fluid in patients with renal dysfunction.

- Intra-aortic balloon pumping (IABP) – This is done for hemodynamic stabilization in the patient with CPE.

- Diet – A low-sodium diet is used to minimize fluid retention.

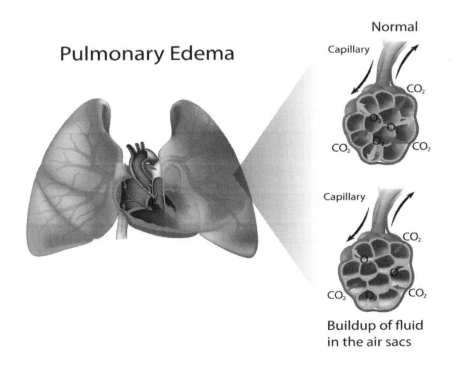

Pulmonary Edema

Normal

Capillary

Buildup of fluid in the air sacs

Medical Management

Medical management of CPE involves three main goals. These include:

- Preload Reduction – Reducing pulmonary venous return to decrease pulmonary capillary hydrostatic pressure and fluid transudation in the alveoli and interstitium

- Afterload Reduction – Reducing systemic vascular resistance to increase cardiac output and improve renal perfusion

- Inotropic Support – Maintains adequate blood pressure

Inpatient Care

Once the patient with CPE is stabilized, his or her inpatient care involves maintaining hemodynamic stability. Nursing measures include:

- Monitoring intake and output.

- Evaluating cardiac enzyme levels for MI.

- Assisting with stress testing if ordered.

- Administering necessary medications.

Medications for CPE

- Loop Diuretics – Remove excessive fluid from the body

- Nitroglycerine – Decrease preload

- ACE Inhibitors – Decrease afterload

- Nesiritide – Reduces pulmonary capillary wedge pressure, systemic vascular resistance, and pulmonary artery pressure

Cardiac Surgery

Valve Replacement

A diseased valve can be replaced with a prosthetic heart valve to reduce the morbidity and mortality of valvular conditions. The four valves of the heart are the aortic, mitral, tricuspid, and pulmonary. Valve replacement surgery requires general anesthesia. Open surgery requires an incision above the sternum and a heart-lung bypass machine. Techniques include laparoscopy, percutaneous, and robot-assisted.

- Ring Annuloplasty – During this procedure, the surgeon repairs the ring portion around the valve by sewing a ring of tissue, plastic, or cloth around the valve.

- Valve Repair – During this procedure, the surgeon trims, rebuilds, or shapes one or more leaflets of the diseased valve.

- Mechanical Valve – This is a man-made valve, which is constructed of titanium, ceramic, or stainless steel.

- Biological Valve – This valve is constructed of human or animal tissue, and typically last for 12 to 15 years.

Conditions Requiring Valve Replacement

- Defects in the heart valve that lead to symptoms such as chest pain, syncope, heart failure, and dyspnea.

- The heart valve was damaged due to endocarditis.

- Tests show that the heart valve is affecting overall cardiac function.

- The prosthetic valve is not working well.

Other Conditions Treated with Valve Replacement

- Aortic stenosis

- Aortic insufficiency

- Mitral stenosis

- Mitral regurgitation

- Mitral valve prolapse

- Tricuspid stenosis

- Tricuspid regurgitation

- Pulmonary valve stenosis

- Congenital valve disease

Complications of Valve Replacement Surgery

- Hemorrhage
- Medication reactions
- Pulmonary embolism
- Thrombosis
- Infection
- Myocardial infarction
- Renal failure
- Arrhythmias
- Stroke
- Death

Coronary Artery Bypass Grafting (CABG)

Coronary artery bypass grafting (CABG) is a surgery used for patients with significant coronary artery disease (CAD). The American College of Cardiology (ACC) and the American Heart Association (AHA) recommends class I indications for CABG, which include:

- Stenosis of the proximal LAD and proximal circumflex >70%
- Left main coronary artery stenosis > 50%
- 3-vessel disease in asymptomatic patients or those with mild/stable angina
- 3-vessel disease with proximal LAD stenosis in patients with altered LV function
- 1- or 2-vessel disease and a large area of viable myocardium in patients with stable angina
- Greater than 70% proximal LAD stenosis with either ejection fraction < 50% or demonstrable ischemia on noninvasive testing
- Disabling angina
- Continued ischemia

Coronary artery bypass surgery

Before   **After**

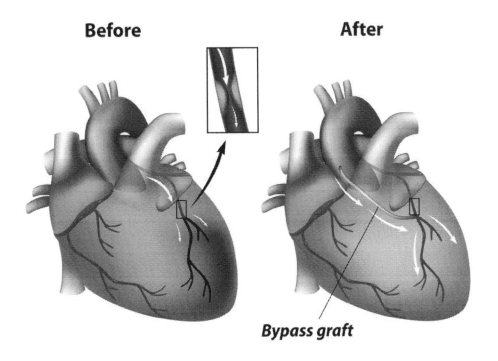

Bypass graft

Before CABG

Pre-procedural evaluation before CAGB involves a detailed patient medical history and physical examination. Routine preoperative studies include:

- Clotting screen
- Complete blood count
- Electrolytes
- Creatinine and BUN
- ECG
- Chest x-ray
- Echocardiogram
- Coronary angiography (to evaluate the location of the CAD)

Medications

Before CABG, the patient is given certain medications to minimize myocardial oxygen demands by heart rate reduction and stabilization of blood pressure. Also, certain drugs are used for anxiety. Typical drugs used include:

- Beta blockers

- Calcium channel blockers

- Nitrates

- Temazepam

- Midazolam

Surgical Monitoring

- ECG

- Pulse oximetry

- Nasopharyngeal temperature

- Urine output

- Gas analysis

- Invasive blood pressure

- Central venous access

- Neurological monitoring

- Transesophageal echocardiography

Cardiac Trauma

Blunt cardiac injury (BCI) refers to injury sustained due to blunt heart trauma. This type of injury can lead to silent arrhythmias, cardiac dysfunction, or heart muscle wall rupture. BCI occurs in approximately 20 percent of motor vehicle accidents, and for patients with severe thoracic trauma and multiple injuries, the incidence is much higher. Sequelae of BCI includes myocardial infarction, ventricular failure, valve damage, embolism, and ventricular rupture.

Signs and Symptoms

- Chest pain

- Palpitations

- Hypotension

American Association for the Surgery of Trauma (AAST) Injury Scale

- Grade I: Blunt cardiac injury with minor ECG changes, such as nonspecific ST and T wave changes, persistent sinus tachycardia, premature ventricular contractions, and premature atrial contractions.

- Grade II: Blunt cardiac injury with ischemic changes or heart block without cardiac failure; or penetrating cardiac wound without tamponade.

- Grade III: Blunt cardiac injury with multifocal ventricular contractions; blunt pericardial laceration; blunt or penetrating injury with septal rupture, papillary muscle dysfunction, pulmonary or tricuspid incompetence, or distal coronary artery occlusion without cardiac failure; or penetrating myocardial wound with tamponade.

- Grade IV: Blunt or penetrating cardiac injury with septal rupture, papillary muscle dysfunction, pulmonary or tricuspid incompetence, or distal coronary artery occlusion that produces cardiac failure; blunt or penetrating cardiac injury with aortic or mitral valve incompetence; and blunt or penetrating cardiac injury of the right ventricle, right atrium, or left atrium.

- Grade V: Blunt or penetrating cardiac injury with proximal coronary artery occlusion; blunt or penetrating left ventricular perforation; or stellate injuries with less than 50 percent tissue loss of the right ventricle, right atrium, or left atrium.

- Grade VI: Blunt avulsion of the heart; or penetrating wound that produces more than 50 percent tissue loss in one or more chambers.

Types of Cardiac Injury

- Pericardial Injury – This results from a direct high-energy impact or an increase in intra-abdominal pressure. The pericardium will rupture and this causes torsion of the great vessels and cardiac evisceration. Treatment involves surgical intervention with median sternotomy.

41

- Valvular Injury – The aortic valve and the mitral valve are the most commonly injured structures, and this leads to left ventricular dysfunction, cardiogenic shock, and pulmonary edema.

- Coronary Artery Injury – Direct high-energy impact can cause arterial thrombosis, with the possibility of chamber rupture, MI, arrhythmia, embolism, or ventricular aneurysm.

- Cardiac Chamber Rupture – This is an often fatal injury that results in pericardial tamponade.

- Myocardial Contusion – This involves direct injury to the heart muscle and usually produces elevated cardiac enzymes and ECG changes.

Diagnosis

- Chest X-ray
- ECG
- Holter monitoring
- Cardiac enzymes
- TTE echocardiogram
- Nuclear medicine scan

Cardiogenic Shock

Cardiogenic shock is decreased cardiac output that leads to tissue hypoxia. This condition is the leading cause of death for patients who suffer AMI, with mortality rates of around 85 percent when the patient does not receive adequate technical care.

Signs and Symptoms

- Hypotension
- Hypovolemia
- Oliguria
- Cyanosis

- Altered mentation

- Mottled, cool extremities

- Faint, rapid peripheral pulses

- Arrhythmias

- JVD

- Peripheral edema

- Extra heart sounds

- Low pulse pressure

- Tachycardia

- Decreased urine output

- Hypotension

Diagnosis

- Metabolic profile

- CBC

- Cardiac enzymes

- ABGs

- BNP

- Lactate

- Echocardiogram

- Chest x-ray

- Coronary angiography (Indicated for patients with MI or ischemia)

- ECG

- Swan-Ganz catheterization

Treatment and Management

- Fluid resuscitation – To treat hypotension and hypovolemia.

- Correction of electrolyte and acid-base abnormalities – This includes acidosis, hypokalemia, and hypomagnesemia.

- Central line placement – To facilitate volume resuscitation and give vascular access for infusions.

- Arterial line – To provide blood pressure monitoring.

- Procedures – PCI or CABG.

Medications

- Diuretics – To decrease edema and plasma volume.

- Inotropic or Vasopressors – To maintain mean arterial pressure (MAP) of 60-65 mmHg.

- Dopamine – Used to improve cardiac contractility and increase myocardial oxygen demand.

- Phosphodiesterase Inhibitors – Used in patients with cardiac pump failure, such as inamrinone.

Cardiomyopathies

Hypertrophic Cardiomyopathy

Hypertrophic cardiomyopathy (HCM) is a genetic condition with a high incidence of sudden death. Characteristic of HCM is myocardial hypertrophy that is often asymmetrical and occurs without an inciting hypertrophic stimulus.

Signs and Symptoms

- Syncope or near syncope

- Dyspnea

- Angina

- Palpitations

- Orthopnea

- Dizziness

- Heart failure

- Sudden cardiac death

- JVD

- Extra heart sounds

- Double carotid arterial pulse

Diagnosis

- ECG

- Genetic testing

- Chest x-ray

- Radionuclide imaging

- Cardiac magnetic resonance imaging

- Cardiac catheterization – Done to determine the degree of outflow obstruction, the left ventricle characteristics, and cardiac hemodynamics.

- Electrophysiological studies

ECG Findings

- Axis deviation

- ST-T wave abnormalities

- Sinus bradycardia

- Atrial enlargement

- P-R prolongation

- Bundle branch block (BBB)

- Prominent or abnormal Q wave

Treatment and Management

- Beta blockers
- Calcium channel blockers
- Antitussives
- Mitral valve replacement
- Permanent pacemaker implantation
- Cardioverter defibrillator implantation
- Catheter septal ablation
- Left ventricular myomectomy

Dilated Cardiomyopathy

Dilated cardiomyopathy is a progressive heart muscle disease that is characterized by ventricular enlargement and LV contractile dysfunction. Both ventricles may be dilated with this heart condition, and it is the most frequent reason for heart transplantation.

Signs and Symptoms

- Fatigue
- Orthopnea
- Dyspnea on exertion
- Edema
- Tachypnea
- Tachycardia
- Hypertension
- JVD
- Pulmonary edema
- S3 gallop
- Hepatomegaly

- Cyanosis

- Nail clubbing

Normal heart   Dilated cardiomyopathy

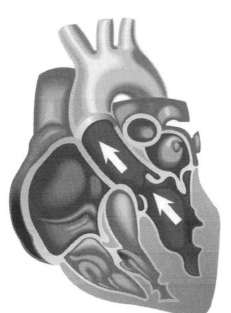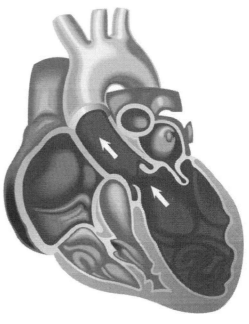

Diagnosis

- CBC

- Metabolic panel

- Cardiac biomarkers

- Thyroid function tests

- BNP

- Chest x-ray

- Echocardiogram

- ECG

- Cardiac magnetic resonance imaging

Treatment and Management

- Left ventricular assist devices

- Ventricular restoration surgery

- Cardiac resynchronization therapy

- Automatic cardioverter defibrillator implantation

- Heart transplantation

Medications

- Beta blockers

- ACE inhibitors

- ARBs

- Diuretics

- Cardiac glycosides

- Aldosterone antagonists

- Vasodilators

- Antiarrhythmics

- Human B-type natriuretic peptide

- Inotropic agents

- Anticoagulants (for select patients)

Restrictive Cardiomyopathy

Restrictive cardiomyopathy (RCM) is a rare heart condition characterized by diastolic dysfunction and restricted ventricular filling. The course of RCM disease varies from patient to patient, and the prognosis is poor. RCM can be idiopathic or associated with other endomyocardial disease. Later in the disease, the abnormal heart function affects the liver, lungs, and other body systems. The most common cause of RCM is amyloidosis and scarring (idiopathic myocardial fibrosis). Other causes include carcinoid heart disease, endomyocardial fibrosis, hemochromatosis, scleroderma, and heart tumors.

Signs and Symptoms

- Gradually worsening dyspnea
- Fatigue
- Exercise intolerance
- Paroxysmal nocturnal dyspnea
- Ascites
- Chest pain
- Palpitations
- Atrial fibrillation
- Orthostatic hypotension
- Syncope and near syncope
- Decreased urine output

Diagnosis

- Chest x-ray
- ECG
- Chest CT
- Cardiac catheterization
- Coronary angiography
- Echocardiogram
- Serum iron studies
- Nuclear heart scan
- MRI of the heart
- Serum or urine protein tests

Treatment and Management

- Aspirin

- Anticoagulants

- Diuretics

- Antiarrhythmics

- Steroids

- Chemotherapy (in select cases)

- Heart transplantation

Dysrhythmias

Cardiac Cells

The heart can pump in a rhythmic action because it has electrical (conductive) cells, which initiate an impulse that is passed along the entire cardiac conduction system. Various contracting (mechanical) cells respond to the electrical impulse, causing the heart muscle to contract and pump blood.

- Automaticity – This is the physiological property of the cardiac cells that allow them to send the electrical impulse. This action occurs when cells alter their membranes and attract sodium (NA+) into them.

- Excitability – This is the physiological property of the cardiac cells that allows the cell to respond to the impulse.

- Conductivity – This is the physiological property of the cardiac cells that allows each cell to put off the impulse.

- Contractility – This is the physiological property of cardiac cells that allows the cell to pump blood in response to the stimulus.

The Conduction System

The conduction system consists of the:

- Sinoatrial (SA) node

- Atrioventricular (AV) node

- Intra-atrial pathway

- Intermodal pathway

- Bundle of His

- Right and left bundle branches

- Purkinje fibers

Cardiac Conduction Disturbances

Standard ECG and rhythm strips – These are recordings at a speed of 25 mm/sec. The vertical axis measures distance, and the smallest divisions are approximately 1mm long. The horizontal axis measures time, with each division representing 0.04 sec/mm.

- P wave – This represents atrial depolarization and is < 0.10 seconds wide and < 3 mm high.

- PR interval – The PR interval is 0.12 to 0.20 seconds.

- QRS complex – This represents ventricular depolarization and measures 0.06 to 0.10 seconds wide.

- Q wave – This is < 0.04 seconds wide and < 3 mm deep.

- R wave – This is < 7.5 mm high.

- QT interval – This varies with sex and rate, but is typically 0.33 to 0.42 seconds.

- T wave – This represents ventricular repolarization, and measures < 5 mm high.

- U wave – This represents ventricular after-potential, and is any deflection after the T wave.

- Prominent U wave – This can indicate hypokalemia, hypercalcemia, thyrotoxicosis, and therapy with certain medications.

- Inverted U wave – This can indicate acute coronary ischemia, hypertension, ventricular strain, or intracranial hemorrhage.

Bradycardia

Bradycardia is a slow heartbeat, and it has four classifications, by dysfunction of the heart pacemaker: escape rhythms, parasympathetic nervous system stimulation, and drug-induced. Etiologies of sinus bradycardias include medications, myocardial infarction, coronary ischemia, age, illness, and metabolic disorders. Treatment is atropine 0.5 – 1 mg IV, which can be repeated in five minute intervals for up to a total of 3 mg. The CCRN must monitor for adequate tissue perfusion, and give vasosuppressor support as required.

Tachycardia

Tachycardia is a fast heartbeat, which is often related to an attempt to compensate for change in cardiac output. Ventricular or wide tachycardias are treated with amiodarone bolus of 150 mg, which can be flowed by a continuous infusion at 1 mg/minute. Atrial fibrillation with rapid ventricular response is treated with a calcium channel blocker or a beta blocker. Diltiazem is given in an initial bolus of 0.25 mg/kg over two minutes and then at 10 mg/hr.

Normal and Pathological Electrocardiograms

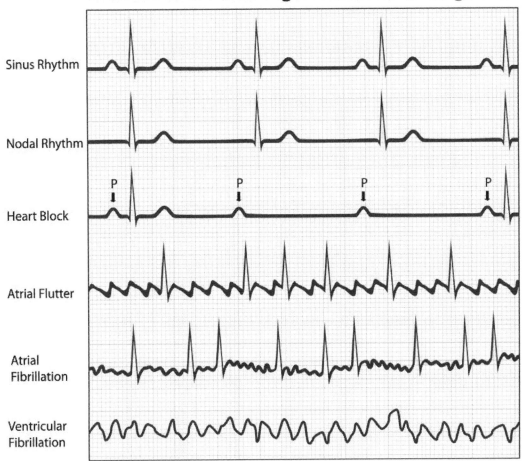

Myocardial Conduction System Defects

- Bundle Branch Block – When there is a block in the right or left branches, impulses must travel to the affected side by way of a detour. This indicates that one of the ventricles is contracting a fraction of a second slower than the other. A bundle branch block usually does not cause any symptoms, and no treatment is usually necessary.

- First Degree Heart Block – With this dysrhythmia, the electrical impulse moves through the AV node slowly, and the heart beat is at a slow rate. This causes dizziness for some patients. Drugs used to treat first degree heart block include beta blockers, calcium channel blockers, and digoxin.

- Second Degree Heart Block – This occurs when electrical impulses from the atria do not reach the ventricles, and there is dropped beats on the ECG. With

Mobitz Type 1 block (Wenckebach), there are not usually symptoms, but the patient may have dyspnea on exertion, syncope, palpitations, and/or chest pain. Mobitz Type 2 block often requires a pacemaker, and the patient also experiences symptoms.

- Third Degree Heart Block – Also called complete heart block, this dysrhythmia occurs when the electrical impulse does not pass from the hearts atria to the ventricles at all. Secondary pacemaker cells must take over, and this causes the ventricles to contract at a slower rate. Most third degree heart block occurs from an existing heart condition, an injury during heart surgery, or as a side effect of certain medications.

- Long Q-T Syndrome – If the Q-T interval is longer than normal, it is referred to as a prolonged Q-T interval or long Q-T syndrome. This is an uncommon genetic disorder that often affects children and young adults. Some patients with this dysrhythmia do not have symptoms, but others experience syncope and palpitations. Treatment for LQTS is beta blockers, an implantable defibrillator, and surgery.

- Heart Failure - Heart failure occurs when there is an abnormality of cardiac function, and the ventricles fail to pump blood at an appropriate rate. According to the AHA, heart failure affects approximately 5.7 million of people in the U.S and causes more hospitalizations than all types of cancer. Also, heart failure accounts for around 35 percent of cardiovascular deaths. The prevalence of heart failure increases with age, with 10 percent of people over the age of 75 affected.

Signs and Symptoms

- Orthopnea

- Dyspnea at rest and on exertion

- Fatigue and weakness

- Pulmonary edema

- Tachycardia

- Chest pain

- JVD

- Anorexia and weight loss

- Extra heart sounds

- Rales and wheezing

- Weak, thread, and/or rapid pulse

- Hepatojugular reflux

- Ascites and hepatomegaly

- Central or peripheral cyanosis

Diagnosis with Framingham Criteria

The Framingham criteria are used for the diagnosis of heart failure. It consists of major and minor criteria.

Major Criteria

- Weight loss of 4.5 kg in five days in response to treatment

- Paroxysmal nocturnal dyspnea

- JVD

- Pulmonary edema

- S3 gallop

- Rales

- Hepatojugular reflux

- Central venous pressure greater than 16 cm

- Radiographic cardiomegaly

Minor Criteria

- Nocturnal cough

- Exertional dyspnea

- Pleural effusion

- Bilateral ankle edema

- Tachycardia
- Decreased vital capacity

Testing for HF

- CBC
- UA
- Electrolytes
- Renal and liver function studies
- Lipid profile
- TSH
- BNP
- N-terminal pro-B-type natriuretic peptide
- ECG
- Chest x-ray
- 2D Echo
- Nuclear imaging
- Pulse oximetry
- ABGs
- Maximal exercise testing
- Nuclear imaging

Treatment and Management

- Oxygen
- Noninvasive positive pressure ventilation
- Sodium and fluid restriction
- Physical activity as appropriate
- Weight monitoring

- Electrophysiological intervention

- Valve replacement or repair

- Revascularization procedures

- Extracorporeal membrane oxygenation

- Heart transplantation

Medications

- Diuretics

- Vasodilators

- Anticoagulants

- Beta blockers

- Inotropic agents

- Digoxin

Hypertensive Crisis

Poorly controlled hypertension can lead to end-organ dysfunction (EOD), and a hypertensive crisis can result in serious consequences for the patient. Neurological EOD from uncontrolled BP include cerebral vascular accident, subarachnoid hemorrhage, hypertensive encephalopathy, and intracranial hemorrhage. Cardiovascular consequences include myocardial infarction, acute pulmonary edema, left ventricular dysfunction, and aortic dissection. Also, the kidneys are also affected by elevated blood pressure.

Accelerated hypertension and malignant hypertension are both considered hypertensive emergencies. A patient with malignant hypertension usually always has retinal papilledema, and may have encephalopathy, left ventricular failure, confusion, impaired renal function, hematuria, intravascular coagulation, and weight loss.

Diagnosis

- For patients in hypertensive crisis, testing may be done. This includes:
- CBC
- Peripheral blood smear (to exclude Microangiopathic Anemia)
- Electrolytes
- BUN and creatinine
- Urinalysis
- Toxicology screen
- Pregnancy test
- Endocrine studies
- CT of the head (for patients with neurological signs)
- ECG (for patients with chest pain)
- Chest x-ray

Treatment and Management

The goal of treatment in a hypertensive crisis is to restore BP to normal. Patients with systolic BP > 200 mmHg or diastolic BP > 120 mmHg without symptoms should have medical therapy and close monitoring. Commonly used medications include:

- Sodium Nitroprusside – Given IV and titrated from minute to minute in the intensive care setting.
- Labetalol – An alpha- and beta-blocking agent preferred for patients with end-stage renal disease (ESRD) and those with acute dissection. A bolus of 10 to 20 mg is given initially, or the drug is infused at 1 mg/min until BP is normalized.
- Clevidipine – A dihydropyridine calcium channel blocker that is administered via IV at 1 to 2 mg/hour and titrated.
- Fenoldopam – This peripheral dopamine-1-receptor agonist is given as an initial IV dose of 1 µg/kg/min and titrated every 15 minutes.

Cardiovascular Emergencies

Cardiovascular emergencies related to elevated blood pressure include:

- Acute Coronary Syndrome –Nitroglycerine and beta blockers

- Acute HF –IV or SL nitroglycerine and IV enalaprilat

- Aortic Dissection –Nicardipine, labetalol, esmolol, and nitroprusside

Neurologic Emergencies

Rapid BP reduction is necessary for neurologic emergencies, including:

- Ischemic stroke – Labetalol and nicardipine

- Hypertensive encephalopathy – Esmolol, labetalol, and nicardipine

- Acute intracerebral hemorrhage – Labetalol, nicardipine, and esmolol

Hypovolemic Shock

Hypovolemic shock occurs when there is rapid fluid loss and multiple organ failure due to inadequate fluid volume and poor perfusion. This condition is often secondary to hemorrhage secondary to burns, GI bleeding, rupture of an abdominal aortic aneurysm, or trauma.

Signs and Symptoms

- Weakness and fatigue

- Pale, cool, clammy skin

- Confusion

- Agitation or anxiety

- Tachypnea

- Diaphoresis

- Decreased or no urine output

- Unconsciousness

- Low blood pressure

- Weak, rapid, thread pulse

- Low body temperature

Diagnosis

- Electrolytes

- BUN and creatinine

- CBC

- CT, US, and/or x-ray of injured area

- Echocardiogram

- Endoscopy

- Swan-Ganz catheter

Complications

- Brain damage

- Kidney damage

- Myocardial infarction

- Gangrene of extremities

- Death

Treatment and Management

- IV line to replace fluids and/or blood.

- Medications, such as dopamine, epinephrine, dobutamine, and norepinephrine.

- Urinary catheter to monitor urine output.

Interventional Cardiology

Cardiac Catheterization

Cardiac catheterization provides intracardiac pressure and oxygen saturation measurements, as well as cardiac output evaluation. This procedure is done to diagnose cardiac diseases. The indications for cardiac catheterization include:

- Assessment of myocardial and valvular disorders to determine if surgical correction is necessary.

- Identification of the severity of CAD and evaluation of LV function.

- Determination of CAD with patients who have atypical chest pain.

Before the cardiac catheterization, the CCRN should explain the risks and benefits to the patient, obtain written consent, and answer all questions from the patient and/or family members. Several preoperative tests and tasks will be done, including a complete history and physical, CBC, blood chemistries, ECG, and chest x-ray. The patient will be NPO for eight hours, and will be medicated with a mild sedative.

Percutaneous Transluminal Coronary Angioplasty (PTCA)

Percutaneous transluminal coronary angioplasty (PTCA) is performed on the patient who has CAD to open one or more blocked coronary arteries. A special catheter is inserted into the coronary artery and a tiny balloon is inflated into the narrowed region of the vessel. The balloon compresses the plaque in the artery to improve blood flow. Fluoroscopy assists the physician to locate the areas of blockages. Also, during the PTCA procedure, a sample of tissue is often taken for microscopic analysis.

Atherectomy

Atherectomy means "removal of plaque." This procedure is done during PTCA when the plaque is calcified or hardened and must be removed in order to keep the artery patent. The catheter inserted has a balloon tip, and there are tiny glades that will cut away the plaque. Some atherectomy procedures are done with a laser, which will vaporize the plaque to remove it.

Stent Placement

Depending on the patient and the situation, the physician may place a stent in the coronary artery during the PTCA procedure. A stent is a tiny, metal coil that keeps the artery open permanently. Once the stent is in place, tissue grows over it within a few days of the procedure. The patient will have to take medications to prevent platelet aggregation after stent placement, such as aspirin, clopidogrel, and/or prasugrel.

Risks of Cardiac Procedures

These include:

- Blood clots
- Bleeding at catheter insertion site (typically the groin)
- Damage to the blood vessel at catheter insertion site
- Infection at the catheter insertion site
- Rupture of the coronary artery
- Myocardial infarction
- Arrhythmias

Nursing Considerations before Cardiac Procedures

- Answer all patient/family/caregiver questions.
- Have the patient sign a consent form.
- Assess for allergies to latex, tape, anesthetics, contrast dyes, and medications.
- Have the patient fast for the specified period of time.
- Remove all of the patient's jewelry, piercings, and body attachments.

Nursing Considerations during Cardiac Procedures

- Assist patient into the specified gown.
- Have the patient empty his or her bladder prior to the procedure.
- Start and IV line and administer fluids/medications as ordered.
- Connect to the ECG monitor.

- Assess and record vital signs.

- Assist physician with the procedure.

Nursing Considerations after Cardiac Procedures

- Have the patient remain flat in the bed for specified amount of time after the procedure.

- Monitor vital signs and distal pulses.

- Assess insertion site.

- Assess for chest pain/pressure and pain at the insertion site or affected leg/arm.

- Assist patient with bedpan or urinal as needed.

- Administer pain medication as ordered.

Aortic Dissection

Aortic dissection occurs when there is separation of the layers within the aortic wall. The aorta is made of three layers of tissue, and the dissection begins with a tear in the inner layer, typically the ascending or descending thoracic aorta. If the tear occurs in the inner layer of the aortic wall, the blood is channeled into the aorta wall that separates the layers of tissue. This causes pressure on the aortic wall, so it ruptures. Aortic dissection result in high mortality, despite advancements in diagnostic and treatment modalities.

Causes of Aortic Dissection

- Hypertension

- Atherosclerosis

- Trauma

- Cystic medial disease

- Connective tissue disorders

- Bicuspid aortic valve

- Aortitis

- Thoracic aneurysm

- Coarctation of the aorta

- Hypovolemia

- Polycystic kidney disease

Signs and Symptoms

- Severe chest pain of sudden onset described as "ripping" or "tearing"

- Syncope

- Neck and/or jaw pain

- Tingling and/or numbness of the extremities

- Pain and/or weakness of the extremities

- Confusion

- Hemoptysis

- Dyspnea

- Horner syndrome (miosis, ptosis, and anhidrosis)

- Abdominal pain (abdominal aorta)

- Fever

- Anxiety and agitation

- Dysphagia

- Hypertension or hypotension

- Diastolic murmur

- JVD

- ECG

- Chest x-ray

- Ultrasound

- Echocardiogram

- CT

- CBC

- Chemistry studies

- Cardiac markers

Treatment and Management

Acute aortic dissection is treated surgically for most patients. The area of the aorta that is torn will be resected and replaced with a graft. Medical management involves decreasing or maintaining blood pressure and managing pain (narcotics).

Thoracic Aortic Aneurysm

A thoracic aortic aneurysm (TAA) is a weakened, bulging area in the aorta wall, resulting in a ballooning of greater than 50 percent of the normal width (diameter). This aneurysm is located in the chest area, and the descending thoracic aorta is the most common location for a TAA. The three types of TAA are ascending thoracic aneurysm, aortic arch thoracic aneurysm, and descending thoracic aneurysm.

Causes of Ascending Thoracic Aortic Aneurysm

- Genetic disorders

- Atherosclerosis

- Cystic medial degeneration

- Infection

Causes of Aortic Arch Thoracic Aneurysm

- Atherosclerosis

- Takayasu's arteritis

Causes of Descending Thoracic Aortic Aneurysm

- Atherosclerosis

- Advancing age (greater than 55 years)

- Genetic factors

- Hyperlipidemia

- Diabetes

- Male gender

- Smoking

Signs and Symptoms

- Chest, neck, and/or back pain

- Swelling of the neck, head, and/or arms

- Heart failure

- Wheezing and coughing

- Dyspnea

- Dysphagia

Diagnosis

- CT

- MRI

- Echocardiogram

- Chest x-ray

- Arteriogram

Treatment and Management

Treatment of a thoracic aorta aneurysm depends on the patient's age, overall health, and medical history, as well as signs and symptoms. Treatments include:

- Monitoring for size

- Medication to control blood pressure and lipids

- Surgery

Abdominal Aortic Aneurysm (AAA)

When the wall of the aorta in the abdomen weakens, an abdominal aortic aneurysm (AAA) can develop. This is often common in geriatric men, and a ruptured AAA is often fatal due to massive blood loss. The symptoms include tearing back pain, pulsating abdominal mass, and hypovolemic shock.

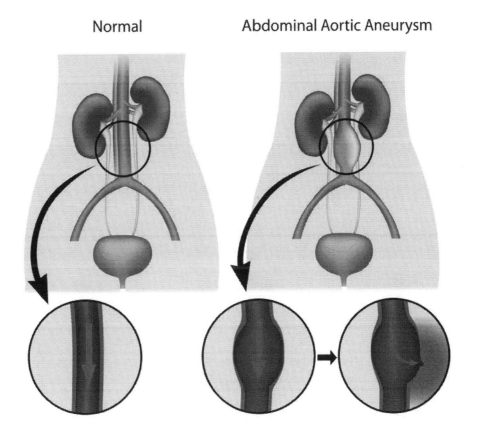

Congenital Heart Defects

Congenital heart defects are present at birth and constitute problems with the heart's structure. The defect can involve the interior walls of the heart, the arteries and veins, and/or the valves inside the heart. The most common type, congenital heart defects, affects around 35,000 infants in the U.S. each year.

Types of Congenital Heart Defects

- Septal Defects – These are holes in the heart. The septum separates the left and right chambers of the heart. A hole in this structure will allow blood to mix between the two sides.

- Atrial Septal Defect (ASD) – This is a hole in part of the septum that separates the two upper heart chambers (atria). Small ASDs are not usually a problem and will close as the child grows. Medium and large ASDs require open heart surgery for repair.

- Ventricular Septal Defect (VSD) – This is a hole in the part of the septum that separates the two lower heart chambers (ventricles). Small VSDs are likely to close on their own, but large ones require surgical intervention.

- Patent Ductus Arteriosus (PDA) – This is a common heart defect that involves abnormal blood flow between the aorta and the pulmonary artery. The ductus arteriosus should close immediately after birth, but for some infants, it remains patent. PDA is usually corrected with surgery, but small PDAs can close without intervention.

- Valve Stenosis – This defect occurs when the flap of the valve stiffens and fuses together, creating a problem with blood flow. The most common is pulmonary valve stenosis.

- Valve Atresia – This defect occurs when the valve does not form correctly and does not have a hole for blood to pass through.

- Valve Regurgitation – With this defect, the valve does not close tightly enough, and blood leaks back through.

- Tetralogy of Fallot – This is a complex heart defect where there is pulmonary valve stenosis, a large VSD, an overriding aorta, and right ventricular hypertrophy. Babies with this defect will need open heart surgery and lifelong medical care.

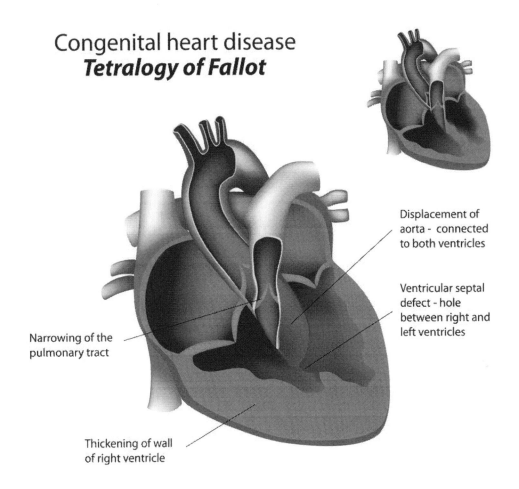

Congenital heart disease
Tetralogy of Fallot

Displacement of aorta - connected to both ventricles

Ventricular septal defect - hole between right and left ventricles

Narrowing of the pulmonary tract

Thickening of wall of right ventricle

Surgery for Heart Defects

Open heart surgery to repair or correct a heart defect is done when the condition cannot be fixed with a catheter procedure. The surgeon performs surgery to:

- Repair or replace heart valves
- Close holes in the septum
- Widen openings or arteries
- Repair complex defects

Aortic Coarctation

Aortic coarctation is narrowing of the aorta, which is most often distal to the origin of the left subclavian artery. This deformity leads to a prominent in-folding that often extends around the entire area of the aorta.

Signs and Symptoms

- Infancy and toddler years – HF, acidosis, poor blood perfusion to lower body.

- Childhood and later years – Possibly no signs and symptoms, but may have headache, hypertension, muscle weakness, cold feet, and nose bleeds.

Physical Findings

- The diagnosis of coarctation is usually made upon physical examination. Common physical findings include:

- Characteristic murmurs – Such as continuous or late systolic murmur, aortic ejection sound, diastolic murmur of aortic regurgitation, and/or bilateral collateral arterial murmurs.

- Differences in upper and lower extremity arterial pulses and blood pressures.

Diagnosis

- Chest x-ray – Findings vary with each patient.
- Barium esophagography
- Echocardiogram
- ECG
- Cardiac catheterization

Treatment and Management

- Infusion of prostaglandin E1 – To open the ductus arteriosus.

- Correction of existing acidosis.

- Administration of diuretics and digoxin (for HF and increased afterload).

- Resection of the coarctation site

- Patch aortoplasty

Pulmonary

Management of the patient's airway is an important function of the CCRN. The organs, muscles, and tissues require oxygen for viability and to prevent complications. The purpose of the pulmonary system is to move oxygen through the body and eliminates carbon dioxide from the body. This section covers the pulmonary system and management of the critically ill patient with pulmonary and other conditions.

Anatomy and Physiology

Terms

- Apnea - When breathing stops.

- Asphyxia - Lack of oxygen.

- Atelectasis - Incomplete lung expansion.

- Auscultation - Listening to lung sounds.

- Bronchiole - Small division of the bronchial tree.

- Cyanosis - Bluish discoloration of the skin or lips.

- Dyspnea - Shortness of breath.

- Epistaxis - Nose bleed.

- Hemoptysis - Coughing up blood.

- Hypoxia - Reduced oxygenation of the tissue.

- Intubation - Insertion of a tube.

- Lavage - Washing out.

- Orthopnea - Shortness of breath when lying flat.

- Pleura - Lining that covers the lungs.

- Pleuritis - Inflammation of the pleura.

- Rhinorrhea - Drainage from the nose.

- Tachypnea - Rapid respiratory rate.

Human Respiratory System

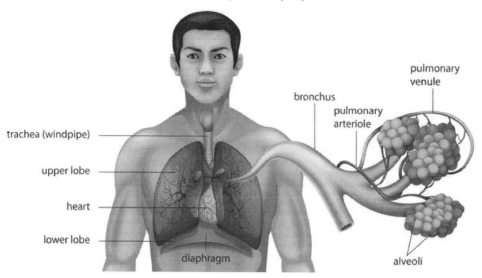

Respiratory Assessment

- Rhythm: Regular or irregular

- Breath sounds: Present and equal vs. diminished or absent

- Chest expansion: Adequate and equal vs. unequal and inadequate

- Effort of breathing: No use vs. use of accessory muscles

Upper Airway

- Nose and mouth

- Nasopharynx (upper part of the throat behind the nose)

- Oropharynx (area of the throat behind the mouth)

- Larynx (voice box)

- Epiglottis (valve that protects the trachea opening)

Lower Airway

- Trachea (windpipe)

- Carina (area where trachea branches into bronchi)

- Bronchi (right and left primary branches of the trachea leading to lungs)

- Bronchioles (small branches of bronchi)

- Alveoli (small airway structures that diffuse oxygen from the respiratory system)

Breathing Muscles and Lung Expansion

- Pleura - Two smooth layers of lung tissue that allow frictionless movement across one another.

- Diaphragm - Primary muscle of respiration that separates the thoracic cavity and is under involuntary control, for the most part.

- Intercostal muscles - Structures between the ribs that contract during inhalation and expand the thoracic cage.

Mechanical Ventilation

Many patients in the intensive care setting require assistance with ventilation. Mechanical ventilation is either invasive or noninvasive. Also called noninvasive positive pressure ventilation (NPPV), noninvasive mechanical ventilation provides adequate oxygenation and ventilation. This is used when the patient has a good respiratory drive but needs assistance keeping the airway patent. Two types of NPPV are continuous positive airway pressure (CPAP) and biphasic positive airway pressure (BIPAP). The use of these measures can reduce the need for intubation, decrease the length of hospital stay, and decrease mortality.

Invasive mechanical ventilation requires the use of an endotracheal tube (ET), which is connected to a ventilator. This is required for patients who are unconscious, in acute respiratory distress, have hemodynamic instability, or those who cannot protect their airway. The two common modes of invasive mechanical ventilation are volume control and pressure control. With a volume control device, the machine controls the amount of tidal volume of inspiration. The physician or nurse can set the tidal volume, respiratory rate, and positive end-expiratory pressure (PEEP). As for pressure control, the ventilator will let the patient determine his or her own tidal volume, but the ventilator must be set to control the PEEP and the respiratory rate.

Pathophysiology

ARDS

Acute respiratory distress syndrome (ARDS) is a critical condition. With this syndrome, there is a buildup of fluid in the alveoli, and the fluid inhibits oxygen from entering the bloodstream. Also, the fluid causes decreased lung expansion. ARDS often occurs along with liver or kidney failure.

Causes of ARDS

- Inhalation of chemicals

- Aspiration of vomitus

- Pneumonia

- Septic shock

- Lung transplant

- Trauma

Signs and Symptoms

- Dyspnea

- Increased respiratory rate

- Hypotension

- Cyanosis

- Abnormal breath sounds (crackles and wheezes)

Diagnosis

- ABG

- CBC

- Chemistry studies

- Chest x-ray

- Bronchoscopy

- Sputum cultures

To rule out HF, an echocardiogram and Swan-Ganz catheter may be used.

Complications of ARDS

- Pulmonary fibrosis

- Pneumothorax

- Organ failure

- Ventilator-associated pneumonia

Treatment and Management

In the intensive care setting, the goal of treatment is breathing support and prevention of complications. The ventilator is used to deliver a high concentration of oxygen and continued positive end-expiratory pressure (PEEP). The patient will be sedated with medications during this, and other medications will be used to reduce inflammation, remove fluid, and treat infections.

Acute Pulmonary Embolus

An acute pulmonary embolus (PE) arises from a deep venous thrombi of the lower extremities. However, a PE can originate in the renal, pelvic, or upper extremity veins or the right heart chambers. The thrombi travel from the vein and lodge at the bifurcation of the main pulmonary artery or in the lobar branches.

Pulmonary Embolism

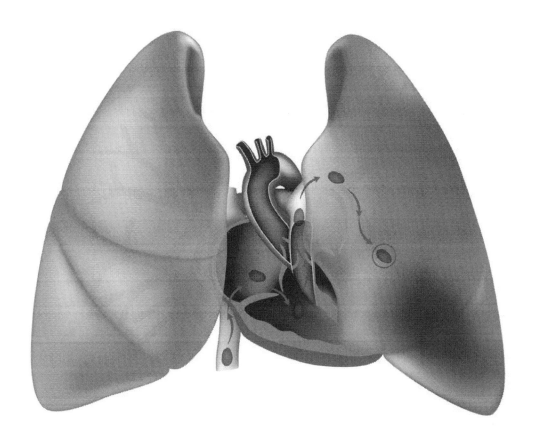

Signs and Symptoms

- Pleuritis-related chest pain
- Dyspnea
- Hypoxia
- Syncope
- Wheezing
- Cough
- Abdominal pain

- Seizures

- Hemoptysis

- Flank pain

- Altered consciousness

- Fever

- New onset of atrial fibrillation

Physical Findings

- Tachycardia

- Rales

- Tachypnea

- Fever

- Diaphoresis

- S3 or S4 gallop

- Lower extremity edema

- Cyanosis

Diagnosis

- Routine laboratory tests (to exclude other diagnoses)

- D-dimer

- WBC

- ABG

- BNP

- Serum troponin levels

- Computed tomography angiography (CTA)

- Chest x-ray

- VQ scan (When CT is not available or is contraindicated)

- Echocardiogram
- Venography (for diagnosing DVT)

Treatment and Management

Diagnostic evaluation should not delay anticoagulation therapy. Medications include:

- Unfractionated heparin
- Low-molecular-weight heparin
- Factor Xa inhibitors
- Fondoparinux
- Warfarin
- Alteplase
- Reteplase
- Urokinase
- Streptokinase

Acute Respiratory Failure

Acute respiratory failure (ARF) occurs when the pulmonary system fails to provide oxygen and/or eliminate carbon dioxide. Hypoxemic respiratory failure (type I) is characterized by a low arterial oxygen tension ($P_a O_2$) of less than 60 mm Hg, and is associated with all acute lung diseases. Hypercapnea-related respiratory failure (type II) is characterized by a $PaCO_2$ higher than 50 mm Hg, and can be caused by neuromuscular disease, drug overdose, COPD, and asthma.

Causes of ARF

- Brain stem tumors and abnormalities
- Narcotic or sedative overdose
- Myxedema
- Chronic metabolic alkalosis

- Guillain-Barre syndrome

- COPD

- Asthma

- Cystic fibrosis

- Myasthenia gravis

- Muscular dystrophy

- Kyphoscoliosis

- Morbid obesity

- Cardiogenic pulmonary edema

- Aspiration pneumonia

- Pulmonary hemorrhage

- Pulmonary fibrosis

- Granulomatous lung disease

- Bronchiectasis

- Pulmonary embolism

Diagnosis
- ABG

- Chest x-ray

- PFT

- ECG

- CBC

- Chemistry panel

Treatment and Management

Hypoxemia is treated to minimize threat to organ function, typically by ventilator support. Mechanical ventilation is used to increase PaO2 and to lower the PaCO2.

Acute Respiratory Infections

CCRNs often are required to treat acute respiratory infections. These infections include acute pneumonia, community-acquired pneumonia (CAP), hospital-acquired pneumonia (HAP), and aspiration pneumonia.

Acute Pneumonia

Acute pneumonia is an infection that affects the alveoli. The seriousness of pneumonia depends on the type of microorganism causing the infection, the patient's age, and their overall health status. Acute pneumonia is more serious for:

- Adults over the age of 65 years.

- Infants and young children.

- Patients with chronic diseases, such as COPD and diabetes.

- Patients with a weak immune system, such as those on chemotherapy or people with HIV/AIDS.

Community-Acquired Pneumonia (CAP)

Community-acquired pneumonia (CAP) is pneumonia that occurs in a patient who has not recently been in the hospital. Risk factors for CAP include an age older than 65 years, chronic conditions, such as diabetes, renal failure, and diabetes, a weak immune system, and antibiotic resistance. CAP can be typical or atypical. The typical microorganisms are *Streptococcus pneumonia, Moraxella catarrhalis*, and *Haemophilius influenzae*. The atypical pathogens include the *Mycoplasma* species and *Chlamydophila pneumoniae*.

Hospital-Acquired Pneumonia (HAP)

Hospital-acquired pneumonia (HAP) was previously known as nosocomial pneumonia, and it is a pneumonia that occurs at least 72 hours after the patient is admitted to the hospital. The pathogens inside the hospital are more antibiotic resistant, so patients are usually treated with two or three different antibiotics.

Signs and Symptoms of Pneumonia

- Cough (may produce yellow, green, or bloody sputum)
- Fever
- Dyspnea
- Chest pain that is worse with coughing or deep breathing
- Sweating
- Clammy skin
- Loss of appetite
- Fatigue and low energy
- Altered mentation

Diagnosis of Pneumonia

- Chest x-ray
- CBC
- ABG
- CT of chest
- Pulse oximetry
- Pleural fluid culture (if fluid is in the pleural space)
- Sputum culture and gram stain
- Bronchoscopy

Treatment and Management of Pneumonia

Treatment depends on the type of pneumonia the patient has, as well as the severity of symptoms.

- Bacterial Pneumonia – Treatment is based on the causative microorganism, but is not delayed for patients with serious illness. The macrolides (azithromycin and clarithromycin), the fluoroquinolones, and doxycycline are first-line therapy. For hospital-acquired pneumonia (HAP), third and fourth generation cephalosporin, carbapenems, aminoglycides, and vancomycin are used. Multiple antibiotics are often given for serious cases.

- Viral Pneumonia – Often caused by influenza A or B, viral pneumonia is often treated with amantadine, oseltamivir, or zanamivir. Other causes of viral pneumonia are H5N1 influenza (avian flu), Hantavirus, SARS coronavirus, adenovirus, and parainfluenza virus.

- Aspiration Pneumonia – Corticosteroids are often used in aspiration pneumonia, but there is no evidence to support the use of antibiotics.

Bronchiolitis

Bronchiolitis is edema of the bronchioles associated with mucus accumulation, usually secondary to a viral pathogen. Bronchiolitis typically affects young children under the age of two years, and is commonly caused by the respiratory syncytial virus (RSV). Other viruses that cause bronchiolitis are the adenovirus, parainfluenza, and influenza. The virus is spread by droplet transmission.

Risk Factors for Bronchiolitis

- Secondhand cigarette smoke

- Age younger than six months

- Crowded living conditions

- Bottle fed

- Being born before 37 weeks gestation

Signs and Symptoms

- Cough

- Wheezing or shortness of breath

- Cyanosis

- Fatigue

- Fever

- Tachypnea

- Intercostal retraction

- Nasal flaring

Diagnosis

- ABG

- Chest x-ray

- RSV test

- Influenza test

Treatment and Management

- Fluids, such as Pedialyte

- Humidified air

- Rest

- Oxygen

- Nebulizers

Air Leak Syndromes

The term "air leak" refers to an abnormal collection of air in the thorax cavity. Air should only be in the airways, lungs, esophagus, and stomach, and if it leaks to other body regions, it is considered abnormal.

Pneumothorax

A pneumothorax occurs when a collection of air enters the space around the lungs and the pressure affects lung expansion when the patient takes a deep breath. A pneumothorax occurs from a gunshot wound, a knife assault, a rib fracture, or a medical procedure. With a spontaneous pneumothorax, a bleb (small air blister) breaks open and sends air into the space around the lung.

Risk Factors for Pneumothorax

- COPD
- Cystic fibrosis
- Asthma
- Whooping cough
- Tuberculosis

Signs and Symptoms

- Sharp chest pain that is worse with inhalation or coughing
- Dyspnea
- Cyanosis
- Chest tightness
- Fatigue
- Tachycardia
- Nasal flaring

Diagnosis

- ABG
- Chest x-ray

Treatment and Management

With a small pneumothorax, the air will reabsorb and the patient will stabilize with rest and oxygen. If possible, the physician may use a needle to pull air from around the lung, allowing it to expand, but if the pneumothorax is large, a chest tube placed between the ribs into the area of air collection will drain the lung so it can re-expand.

Pneumopericardium

Pneumopericardium is a collection of gas or air in the pericardial space. This produces hemodynamic changes, depending on the volume and rate of introduction. Up to 500 ml of gas/air may accumulate in the pericardium without serious effects if it slowly enters the pericardial space. However, a much smaller amount of air will cause serious changes if it is introduced rapidly.

Causes of Pneumopericardium

- Blunt or penetrating chest injury and barotrauma.

- Fistulation between the pericardium and the plural space, bronchial tree, or gastrointestinal tract.

- Microorganisms invading the pericardial sac.

Signs and Symptoms

- "Mill wheel" Murmur – Caused by the gas and fluid in the pericardial space

- Tympany – Heard when the precordium is percussed in the upright position

Diagnosis

- Chest x-ray

- ECG

- CT of chest

- Barium contrast swallow test

- Echocardiogram

Treatment and Management

If tamponade develops, urgent pericardiocentesis is required.

Aspirations

Aspiration usually develops in patients who have intrinsic musculoskeletal disease, nervous system conditions, or gastrointestinal problems. Any patient with dysphagia is at risk for aspiration, as well as young children and persons who abuse substances, such as opiates, benzodiazepines, and/or alcohol.

Aspiration Pneumonia

Aspiration pneumonia occurs when saliva, liquids, food, or vomit is inhaled into the lungs and airways. The causative bacteria depends on the circumstances.

Risk Factors for Aspiration Pneumonia

- Advancing age
- Coma
- Decreased or altered gag reflex
- Stroke or brain injury
- Decreased alertness
- Medication

Complications

- Lung abscess
- Respiratory failure
- Shock
- Bacteremia

Signs and Symptoms

- Fever
- Chest Pain
- Cough with foul-smelling and/or colored sputum

- Fatigue

- Dyspnea

- Wheezing

- Breath odor

- Diaphoresis

- Rales or crackles

- Low O2 saturation

- Tachycardia

Diagnosis

- Chest x-ray

- ABG

- Blood culture

- Sputum culture

- CBC

- Bronchoscopy

Treatment and Management

- Antibiotics

- Supplemental oxygen

- Ventilator support (if necessary)

Foreign Body Aspiration

Aspiration of a foreign body is a life-threatening emergency. The object can become lodged in the trachea or larynx, and can cause complete obstruction of the airway, leading to death. Most often, a foreign body is food, but commonly retrieved items include nuts, seeds, nails, small toys, bone fragments, and dental appliances.

Signs and Symptoms

- Fever

- Dyspnea

- Chest pain

- Hemoptysis

- History of a choking episode

- Sudden onset of coughing, decreased breath sounds, and wheezing

Risk Factors

- Young children

- Patients with psychiatric, musculoskeletal, and/or neurologic disorders

- Old age

- Alcohol or sedative use

- Poor dentition

- Institutionalization

- Recent surgery

Immediate Treatment

When treating an aspiration of a foreign object, if the choking and coughing resolves and the patient does not have any symptoms or signs of infection, report the incident to the attending physician. A chest x-ray may be warranted. Also, bronchoscopy is done to confirm the diagnosis and remove the foreign body from the airway. Antibiotics are usually given as a precautionary measure.

Chronic Lung Disease

Patients with one or more forms of chronic lung disease often end up in the intensive care unit. These conditions include asthma, chronic obstructive pulmonary disease (COPD), chronic bronchitis, and emphysema.

Asthma

Asthma is a condition of hyper-responsive airways. This chronic disease affects as many as 24 million individuals in America, and of these, 7 million are children. The mechanism of inflammation in asthma can be acute or chronic, and the presence of mucus secretion and airway edema contributes to bronchial reactivity and airflow obstruction.

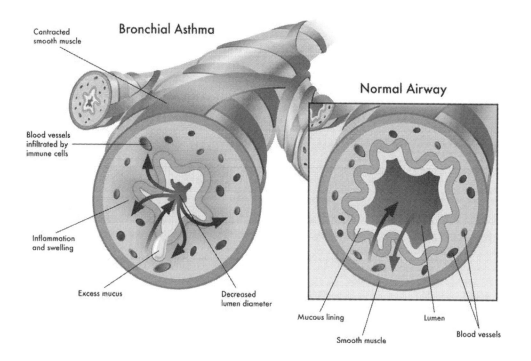

Signs and Symptoms

- Wheezing
- Coughing
- Dyspnea
- Chest tightness
- Chest pain

Diagnosis

- Spirometry with post-bronchodilator response
- Chest x-ray
- Pulse oximetry

Treatment and Management

- Control agents: Inhaled corticosteroids, long-acting bronchodilators, inhaled cromolyn or nedocromil, leukotriene modifiers, and theophylline.
- Quick acting agents: Albuterol and Levalbuterol
- Exacerbations: Inhaled inhaler, nebulizer, and IV corticosteroids.
- Allergen and environmental agent avoidance: Triggers should be avoided, such as animals, dust, mold, and pollen.

COPD

Chronic obstructive pulmonary disorder (COPD) is a term used to describe chronic bronchitis and emphysema. These diseases are the result of trapped air within the lungs due to a loss of pulmonary elasticity and recoil that narrows the airways and leads to inflammation.

Risk Factors for COPD

- Cigarette smoking
- Occupational exposure (coal, silica, asbestos, cadmium, and gold)
- Genetic alpha-1-antitrypsin deficiency

Signs and Symptoms

- Cough
- Wheezing
- Dyspnea that limits activity

- Sputum production

- Cyanosis

- Left-sided heart failure

- Tachypnea

- Use of accessory muscles

- Rales, wheezes, and crackles

Diagnosis

- Chest x-ray

- CT of chest

- ABG

- Serum chemistries

- BNP

- PFT

- Sputum culture

- 2D Echocardiogram (if cor pulmonale is suspected)

Treatment and Management

- Antibiotics (levofloxacin, doxycycline, macrolides, ceftriaxone, and tobramycin)

- Beta agonists (albuterol)

- Anticholinergics (ipratropium)

- Corticosteroids

Chronic Bronchitis

Chronic bronchitis is diagnosed by a productive cough daily for three consecutive months each year over the course of two years. This condition results from chronic inflammation, hyperplasia and hypertrophy of mucus-producing cells, and thickening and scarring of the airways.

Emphysema

Emphysema is destruction of airspace that is distal to terminal bronchioles and the walls of the alveoli. The patient loses elastic recoil of the lung in emphysema, and this is due to destruction of the parenchyma, resulting in inability to properly exhale air.

Pulmonary Hypertension

Pulmonary hypertension (PH) is increased blood pressure in the lung vessels, and it is caused by restriction of the pulmonary arteries, blood clots in the pulmonary vessels, or fibrosis of these vessels. PH is diagnosed when pulmonary artery pressure is greater than 25 mm Hg at rest or 30 mm Hg on exertion.

Types of PH

- Arterial PH – Caused by restriction of the blood arterial vessels leading to the lungs and inside the lungs.

- Venous PH – Caused when the left side of the heart does not pump adequately and pulmonary edema and effusions develop.

- Hypoxic PH – Caused by lung disease, sleep apnea, and pulmonary abnormalities that result in low oxygen levels.

- Thromboembolic PH – Caused by blood clots in the pulmonary vessels.

- Miscellaneous PH – Caused by various diseases, such as sarcoidosis and lung tumors.

Signs and Symptoms

- Dyspnea during activity

- Syncope or near syncope

- Dizziness

- Nonproductive cough

95

- Peripheral edema

- Fatigue

- Graham Steel murmur (pulmonary regurgitation)

- Hepatomegaly and ascites

- Abnormal abdominal-jugular reflex

Diagnosis

- Cardiac catheterization (standard test to confirm PH)

- Chest x-ray

- Antinuclear antibody

- Thyroid function

- BNP

- ECG

- Echocardiogram

- Pulmonary angiography
  CT of lungs

Treatment and Management

- Calcium channel blockers

- Vasodilator

- Septostomy

- Lung transplantation

Thoracic Trauma

Trauma to the thorax is either non-penetrating (blunt) or penetrating, and it is categorized by the site of injury, such as cardiac, pulmonary, esophageal, diaphragmatic, or chest wall.

- Non-penetrating trauma – This type of injury occurs during motor vehicle incidents and accidents. The blunt trauma results in contusions to the heart and/or lungs, as well as the great vessels. The patient will experience dyspnea, tachypnea, tachycardia, pulmonary hemorrhage with hemoptysis, contusions, and vascular rupture.

- Flail chest – When a patient sustains multiple fractures of the ribs, a flail chest occurs. This is compromise in the ability to ventilate due to the patients inability to control the expansion of the thorax cavity. Flail chest is treated with supplemental oxygen, analgesics, possible ventilator support, and chest tube placement.

- Penetrating trauma – With a penetrating injury, the integrity of the thorax cavity is compromised, there is a risk of bleeding and a hemothorax develops. This is treated with chest tube placement.

- Tracheal perforation – This can occur from a non-penetrating or penetrating injury. The symptoms include dyspnea, hemoptysis, hypotension, tachycardia, and mediastinal emphysema. Tracheal perforation is treated with bronchoscopy and primary closure with end-end anastomosis.

Thoracic Surgery

The purpose of thoracic surgery is to correct and treat injured or diseased organs and structures of the thorax, such as the esophagus, trachea, pleura, mediastinum, chest wall, diaphragm, heart, and lungs. The most common diseases that require thoracic surgery are lung cancer, esophageal cancer, chest trauma, emphysema, and lung transplantation.

Invasive Procedures

- Bronchoscopy – Diagnostic bronchoscopy involves the use of a flexible instrument to directly visualize the lung or airway lesion for biopsy. This procedure is performed using topical anesthesia, intravenous sedation, or both.

- Mediastinoscopy – This procedure involves the use of a mediastinoscope (a lighted instrument) to biopsy the lymph nodes for patients with suspected lung cancer or to investigate masses. The instrument passes through a suprasternal incision into the pre-tracheal fascia.

- Anterior mediastinotomy – This is a procedure used to access the sub-aortic lymph nodes to biopsy or remove tumors from the anterior mediastinum, such as thymic lesions. The surgeon makes a short incision in the second or third intercostal space.

- Pleural aspiration and biopsy – This procedure is done to remove fluid from a pleural effusion with a needle and syringe. The material is sent for cytological, biochemical, and/or microbiological analysis.

- Percutaneous biopsy – The percutaneous biopsy is done under CT control to assess tissue for malignancy.

- Video-assisted thoracoscopy – This procedure is done using a camera and scope, so the surgeon can inspect the pleural space, mediastinum, and lung. During this procedure, material is taken from lesions and certain procedures are done, such as those to manage pneumothorax.

- Thoracotomy – This is done when less invasive procedures are not necessary to access the mediastinal lymph nodes, the great vessels, the esophagus, and the lung and pericardium. The posterolateral thoracotomy is done for pulmonary resections, the lateral thoracotomy is used with limited access as necessary, and the anterior thoracotomy is used for open lung biopsy.

- Chest tube insertion – This is done to treat pneumothorax or hemothorax, with the tube inserted at the fourth or fifth intercostal space. The skin is prepared with an antiseptic solution, local anesthetic is give, and the skin incision is made. With forceps and finger technique, the port of entry is widened and the tube is inserted. The chest drain is retained with strong sutures, and the tube is connected to an underwater drainage system, usually high flow and low pressure. To confirm chest tube position, a chest x-ray is required.

- Tracheostomy – This procedure is done through a surgical opening in the trachea. The indications for tracheostomy are respiratory tract obstruction, prolonged mechanical ventilation, tracheobronchial toilet (retained secretions), and laryngeal surgery.

- Median sternotomy – Also called sternal split, this is done to access anterior mediastinal tumors and the lung apices.

Endocrine

The endocrine system is the body's internal regulator. Endocrine glands secrete hormones and enzymes into the blood and ductal structures. The endocrine system regulates growth, sex differentiation, reproduction, metabolism, internal homeostasis, and fluid and electrolyte balance. The major components of the endocrine system are the hypothalamus, pituitary gland, pineal gland, thyroid gland, parathyroid glands, thymus, adrenal glands, pancreas, ovaries, and testes.

Pathophysiology

Diabetes Mellitus

Many ICU patients will have diabetes mellitus (DM), either type 1 (insulin-dependent) or type 2 (non-insulin dependent). Diabetes is a chronic condition where the patient does not produce enough insulin or he or she experiences insulin resistance. When food is ingested, it passes down the GI tract for digestion. Glucose enters the bloodstream from food and this stimulates the pancreas to release a hormone called insulin. Insulin should move glucose from the blood into the liver, muscle, and fat cells so it can be utilized for fuel. However, people with diabetes cannot move the glucose appropriately because their pancreas does not produce any or enough insulin and/or their cells do not respond normally to the insulin.

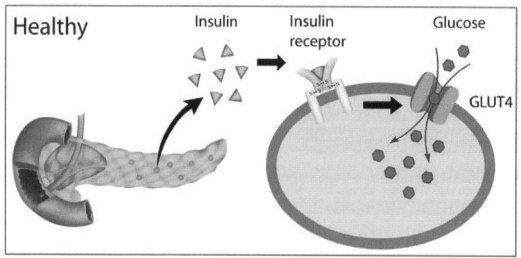

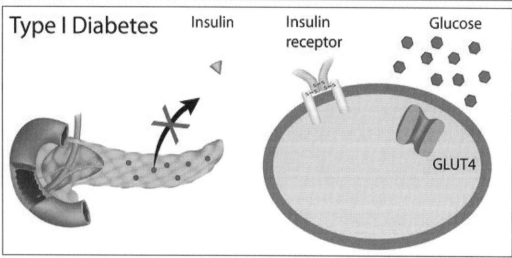

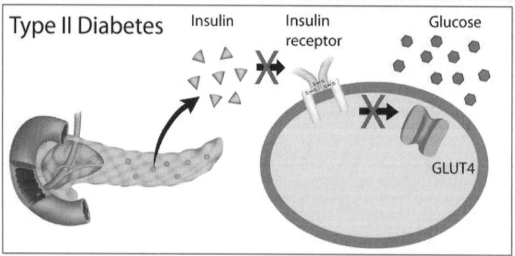

Signs and Symptoms

- Excessive thirst
- Increased urination
- Blurred vision
- Fatigue
- Weight loss
- Hunger

Diagnosis

- Fasting blood glucose level
- Hemoglobin A1C
- UA
- Glucose tolerance test (GTT)

Treatment and Management

There is no cure for type 1 DM, but it can be managed with medications. For patients with type 2 DM, the disease can be reversed with weight loss and appropriate diet. Some patients with type 2 DM are treated with oral agents as well as insulin. Most all patients with type 1 DM require insulin therapy. Common insulin regimens include:

- Split or mixed – NPH rapid-acting (lispro, glulisine, or aspart) or regular insulin before breakfast and dinner.
- Split or mixed variant – NPH rapid-acting or regular insulin before breakfast, rapid-acting or regular insulin before dinner, and NPH before bedtime.
- Multiple daily injections – Long-acting insulin (detemir or glargine) once daily in the am or evening and a rapid-acting insulin before meals and snacks.
- Continuous subcutaneous insulin infusion (CSI) – Rapid-acting insulin infused continuously via insulin pump.

For type 2 DM, various pharmacologic options are available. These include:

- Biguanides

- Meglitinide derivatives

- Sulfonylureas

- Glucagon-like peptide-1 (GLP-1) agonists

- Alpha glucosidase inhibitors

- Thiazolidinedione (TZDs)

- Dipeptidyl peptidase IV (DPP-4) inhibitors

- Selective sodium-glucose transporter-2 (SGLT-2) inhibitors

- Amylinomimetics

- Bile acid sequestrants

Acute Hypoglycemia

Hypoglycemia is defined as a blood glucose level of < 50 mg/dL in men and less than 45 mg/dL in women. Treatment of hypoglycemia in the critical care patient consists of correcting the glucose deficiency and addressing the underlying cause. Administration of glucose is done by IV bolus once the diagnosis is made.

Causes of Hypoglycemia

- Endogenous – Caused by pancreatic tumors, insulinomas, and inborn metabolic errors.

- Exogenous – Caused by insulin secretagogues, insulin excess, alcohol use, oral antidiabetic agents, and certain drugs (pentamidine and salicylates).

- Functional – Caused by dumping syndrome, prolonged muscle use from seizure or exercise, and spontaneous reactive hypoglycemia.

Signs and Symptoms

- Hunger
- Pallor
- Palpitations
- Diaphoresis
- Anxiety
- Nausea
- Weakness
- Restlessness
- Visual disturbances
- Tremors
- Slurred speech
- Staggering gain
- Seizures
- Coma

Diagnosis of Acute Hypoglycemia

- Blood glucose evaluations
- ECG – To screen for cardiac causes.
- Serum drug screen
- Electrolytes
- Renal panel
- Liver function tests

Treatment and Management

Adult acute hypoglycemia is treated with 15 grams of carbohydrates orally when the patient is able to swallow. However, if the patient is unconscious, hypoglycemia is corrected with IV dextrose 25 grams in 50 ml water. After treating and stabilizing the patient, the CCRN must recheck blood glucose regularly, and repeat treatment as necessary. Also, a long-acting carbohydrate food source or meal should be provided.

Diabetes Insipidus

Diabetes Insipidus (DI) is a deficiency of or insensitivity to antidiuretic hormone (ADH). Due to the lack of ADH, the patient is not able to concentrate urine which results in volume depletion, dehydration, and hypernatremia. There are three types of DI: neurogenic, nephrogenic, and dipsogenic.

- Neurogenic DI – Considered central or hypothalamic, neurogenic DI occurs from damage to the posterior pituitary gland from trauma or growths. This leads to insufficient amounts of ADH and an inadequate renal response. Impaired ADH activity causes rapid excretion of dilute urine, decreased urine osmolality, and increased plasma osmolality.

- Nephrogenic DI – This is caused by an inadequate response of the kidneys to ADH, which is peripheral and related to drug toxicity or kidney conditions. This is caused by sarcoidosis, amyloidosis, polycystic kidney disease, multiple myeloma, nephrotoxic drugs, or sickle cell disease.

- Dipsogenic DI – Considered primary polydipsia, this type of DI results from abnormal amounts of water, which suppresses ADH release and causes polyuria. This is caused by psychoses or an impaired thirst mechanism.

Complications

- Dry skin
- Fever
- Dry mucus membranes
- Rapid heart rate
- Sunken eyes or fontanels
- Electrolyte imbalance(s)

- Headache

- Irritability

- Muscle pain

Signs and Symptoms

- Polydipsia

- Polyuria

- Hypernatremia

- Hyperosmolarity

- Mental status changes

- Hypotension

Diagnosis

- MRI of the head

- Total urine output evaluation

- Urinalysis

- Water restriction test – Involves measuring baseline values of ADH, serum, and urine osmolalities, as well as serum sodium concentrations. The urine volume and osmolality is assessed every hour, and the serum's sodium and osmolality is assessed every two hours. If the urine osmolality reaches 600 mOsm/kg, then there is no DI.

- Vasopressin test – Differentiates neurogenic and nephrogenic DI.

Treatment and Management

- Neurogenic DI – Administering vasopressin, desmopressin, or DDAVP.

- Nephrogenic DI – Stopping the medication.

- Anti-inflammatory medications, such as indomethacin.

- Diuretics, such as amiloride or HCTZ.

- Fluid volume replacement by rapid infusion of a hypotonic IV solution.

- Monitoring intake and output.

- Monitoring weight.

- Assess for possible cardiac adverse effects.

Diabetic Ketoacidosis

Diabetic ketoacidosis (DKA) is a life-threatening condition that occurs in diabetic patients. This condition is characterized by ketoacidosis, hyperglycemia, and ketonuria. It occurs in both type 1 and type 2 diabetes; the incidence is around 6 episodes per 1,000 hospitalized patients. DKA is caused by alcohol intoxication, stressful events, failure to take insulin, pregnancy, infection, and undiagnosed diabetes.

Signs and Symptoms

- Weakness and fatigue

- Rapid weight loss

- Decreased appetite

- Nausea and/or vomiting

- Altered consciousness

- Coughing

- Chills

- Cough

- Dyspnea

- Arthralgia

- Chest pain

- Tachycardia

- Hypothermia

- Hypotension

- Dry mucus membranes

- Dry skin

- Tachypnea

- Ketotic breath odor

- Decreased reflexes

Effect of Insulin on Glucose Uptake

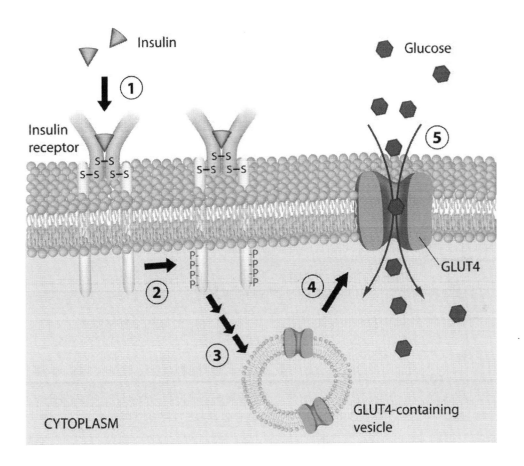

Diagnosis

- Serum glucose

- Electrolytes

- Amylase

- Urinalysis

- ABG

- Bicarbonate level

- BUN and creatinine

- CBC

- Urine and blood cultures

- ECG

- Chest x-ray (to rule out pneumonia)

Treatment and Management

- Fluid resuscitation (0.9% NS 1 liter the first hour, then 300-500 mL per hour for several hours)

- Reversal of ketosis and acidosis

- Reduction of glucose level (IV regular insulin administered at a 10 to 20 unit bolus, followed by continuous infusion of 0.1 unit/kg/hr)

- Electrolyte stabilization

- Identify the underlying cause

- Rapid-acting insulin (aspart, glulisine, and lispro)

- Short-acting insulin (regular)

- Electrolyte infusion (potassium)

- Alkalinizing agents (sodium bicarbonate)

Hyperglycemic Hyperosmolar Non-ketotic Syndrome (HHNK)

Hyperglycemic hyperosmolar non-ketotic syndrome (HHNK) is a serious metabolic condition that occurs in patients with diabetes mellitus. Reduced fluid intake and infection can cause HHNK. It is characterized by elevated glucose levels, hyperosmolarity, and dehydration without ketoacidosis.

Signs and Symptoms

- Glucose level of 600 mg/dL or greater

- Serum osmolality of 320 mOsm/kg or greater

- Profound dehydration

- Bicarbonate concentration of 15 mEq/L or greater

- Serum pH of 7.30 or greater

- Altered level of consciousness

Diagnosis

- Glucose

- Electrolytes

- Blood cultures

- ABG

- Urinalysis

- CT of head (for altered consciousness)

- ECG

Treatment and Management

The main goals of treatment for HHNK are to correct hyperglycemia, to rehydrate the patient, to establish electrolyte homeostasis, and to treat underlying conditions. Therapy includes:

- Airway management

- IV crystalloid administration

- Correction of hyperglycemia with insulin

- Arterial line

- Glucose level monitoring

- ABG monitoring

111

- Correct electrolyte disturbances (hyponatremia, hypernatremia, hypokalemia, hypokalemia, hypochloremia, and/or hyperchloremia)

Syndrome of Inappropriate Secretion of Antidiuretic Hormone (SIADH)

Syndrome of inappropriate secretion of antidiuretic hormone (SIADH) is hyponatremia and hypo-osmolality that occurs from continued secretion or action of antidiuretic hormone (ADH) and impaired water excretion. This occurs in spite of normal plasma volume.

Signs and Symptoms

- Gradual and progressive hyponatremia
- Confusion
- Disorientation
- Delirium
- Muscle weakness
- Tremor
- Hyporeflexia
- Dysarthria
- Cheyne-Stokes respirations
- Seizures
- Coma
- Dilute urine

Diagnosis

- Electrolytes and bicarbonate levels
- Plasma osmolality
- Creatinine and BUN
- Urine osmolality

- Serum uric acid

- Serum cortisol

- TSH

- Chest x-ray

- CT of the head

Treatment and Management

Treatment of SIADH depends on the severity of the condition and the patient's health status and symptoms. If the duration of the hyponatremia is not known in an asymptomatic patient, the SIADH is usually considered to be chronic. Treatment of the underlying cause of SIADH is of utmost importance in the patient's overall care.

Hyponatremia must be corrected at a rate that does not affect neurologic stability, so the serum sodium should rise by 0.5 to 1.0 mEq/hr and not more than 10 mEq in the first 24 hours of treatment. This is accomplished with 3% hypertonic saline solution. Also, medications used include loop diuretics and vasopressin-2 receptor antagonists.

Thyrotoxic Crisis

Also called thyroid storm, thyrotoxic crisis is a severe type of condition associated with hyperthyroidism. This can result in death if not treated within 24 to 48 hours from onset of illness. Thyroid storm occurs in patients who suffer with Grave's disease or those who are undiagnosed or not taking medication appropriately.

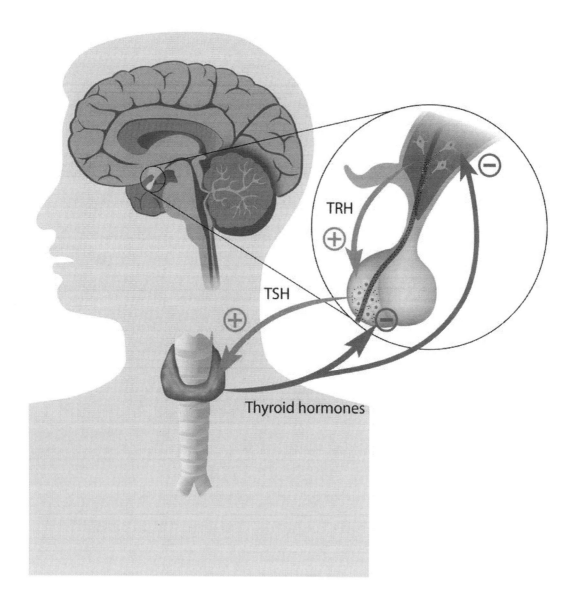

Signs and Symptoms

- High fever
- Palpitations
- Arrhythmias
- Altered respirations
- Fatigue
- Tremors
- Delirium

- Stupor

- Coma

- Loss of temperature regulation

- Warm moist skin

Diagnosis

- TSH

- T3

- T4

- Resin T3 uptake

Treatment and Management

The goals of treatment for the patient with thyrotoxic crisis include treating the cause and inhibiting thyroid hormone biosynthesis to antagonize the peripheral effects from thyroid hormone and to block its release. This is done by administering:

- Propylthiouracil – This is given in a loading dose of 600 mg followed by 200 mg every four hours until thyroid levels regulate

- Methimazole – If the patient cannot take propylthiouracil, this drug is given at 20 mg every four hours

- Sodium Iodine – This is given by IV drip

- Lugol's Solution – This is saturated potassium iodine given orally

- Lithium Carbonate – Used for patients with iodine allergy

- Beta Blockers – Used to slow the heart rate and reduce symptoms

- Supportive Care: Cooling blankets, fluid replacement, and anticoagulation if needed

Myxedema Coma

Myxedema coma is seen in hypothyroid patients and is a life-threatening condition. This can occur due to infection, exposure to cold, trauma, or intake of narcotics or tranquilizers. The patient's metabolism increases due to these stressors, and this depletes stored thyroid hormone from the body.

Signs and Symptoms

- Hypothermia
- Hypotension
- Bradycardia
- Loss of reflexes
- Generalized edema
- Fatigue
- Depressed respirations

Diagnosis

- Thyroid function tests
- CBC
- Electrolytes
- Liver function tests
- Renal function tests
- ABGs
- Blood cultures
- Creatine kinase
- UA
- Cortisol level
- Glucose level

Treatment and Management

The goal of treatment for the patient with myxedema coma include identifying the cause, correcting electrolyte and fluid imbalance, replacing hormones, and supportive care. This involves:

- Administering thyroid hormones – T4 (levothyroxine) is given at 2 mcg/kg of body weight IV over five minutes, and then 100 mcg every day. T3 (liothyronine) is given at 10 to 25 mcg IV every 12 hours until symptoms improve.

- Intubation and mechanical ventilation – If required due to compromised airway.

- Correct cardiac dysrhythmias.

- Continuous cardiac monitoring

- Treat hyponatremia with hypertonic saline and limited water by central venous line.

- Glucose given by IV solution.

- Hydrocortisone 100 mg IV ever eight hours for the first 48 hours to increase glucose and blood pressure.

Hematology/Immunology

CCRNs are often responsible for the care of patients with hematologic and/or immunological conditions. To identify, treat, and manage these patients, the nurse needs a general knowledge of these systems, including hemostasis, formation of cells, coagulation, immune responses, oxygenation, and antibody formation. This section overviews the various conditions and problems associated with the hematologic system and the immune system.

Pathophysiology

The CCRN exam primarily tests your knowledge of coagulation disorders, so that will be the focus of this section.

Patients with coagulation disorders often have a disruption in the normal coagulation processes, so the blood clots more or less than it should. With some hypercoagulable disorders, the patient will develop a secondary bleeding problem when clotting and platelet functions are exhausted (consumptive coagulopathy). Acute coagulation disorders can lead to alteration in blood flow to specific organs and body regions.

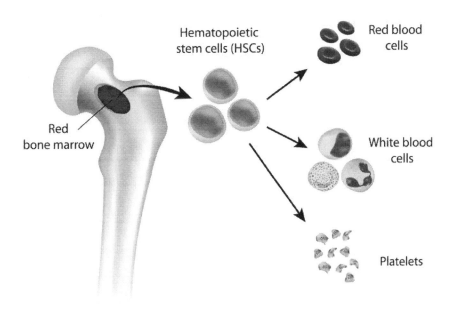

Hemophilia

Hemophilia is a disorder of clotting, and approximately 85 percent of people with this condition are men because these are X-linked recessive disorders. The mother is the carrier of the chromosome, and when the father is normal, the male children have a 50 percent chance of developing hemophilia, and the female children have a 50 percent chance of being a carrier.

Hemophilia results in free bleeding or the propensity to bleed easily, but there are several levels of symptoms. Most patients have to avoid trauma and injury. Treatment for excessive bleeding involves the administration of factor VIII, which is in limited supply.

Types of Hemophilia

- Hemophilia A – Also called classic hemophilia, this is an abnormality or deficiency in clotting factor VIII.

- Hemophilia B – This is a deficiency in clotting factor IX.

- Hemophilia C – Most often affecting Ashkenazi Jews (generally of central or Eastern European descent,) this is a deficiency in clotting factor XI.

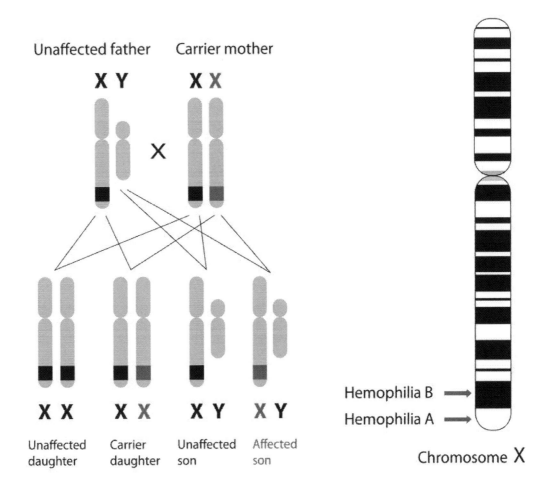

Idiopathic Thrombocytopenic Purpura

Idiopathic thrombocytopenic purpura (ITP) is an autoimmune condition where isolated thrombocytopenia occurs with normal bone marrow. With ITP, there is a decrease in the number of circulating platelets and an absence of toxic exposure to diseases associated with a low platelet count. In the U.S., ITP occurs in 7 out of 10,000 people, affecting females twice as often as males.

Signs and Symptoms

- Menorrhagia
- Epistaxis
- Purpura

121

- Gingival bleeding

- Recent immunization or viral illness (children)

- Bruising

- Petechiae

- GI bleeding

- Retinal hemorrhages

Diagnosis

- CBC

- Peripheral smear

- Coagulation studies

Treatment and Management

- Control of hemorrhage

- Providing oxygen

- IV fluids for hemodynamic stability

- Treating infections

- Platelet transfusions

- Splenectomy (if medications do not help)

Medication Therapy

- Corticosteroids

- Anti-Rh(D) immunoglobulin

- Rituximab

- Eltrombopag

- Romiplostim

Disseminated Intravascular Coagulation

Disseminated intravascular coagulation (DIC) is systemic activation of blood coagulation, which causes deposition of fibrin and microvascular thrombi in the body's various organs. DIC contributes to multiple organ dysfunction syndrome (MODS), as the fibrin contributes to intravascular clot formation and severe bleeding. DIC is secondary to clinical conditions, such as trauma, sepsis, infection, heat stroke, hepatic failure, obstetric complications, transfusion reactions, malignancy, pancreatitis, toxic reactions, and hemorrhagic skin necrosis.

DIC can be acute or chronic. Acute DIC occurs when there is sudden exposure of the patient's blood to pro-coagulants or tissue thromboplastin, causing hemostatic mechanisms to become overwhelmed. Chronic DIC develops when the patient's blood is intermittently or continuously exposed to small amounts of tissue factor, as with large aortic aneurysms or solid tumors.

Diagnosis

There is no one test to diagnose DIC, but the CBC will show moderate or severe thrombocytopenia, and blood smears often show schistocytes. Also, the patient will have long coagulation times, high levels of fibrin, and elevated D-dimer.

- Platelet count
- Global clotting times (aPTT and PT)
- Protein C and anti-thrombin (usually decreased)
- D-dimer

Treatment and Management
- Monitor vital signs.
- Correct hypovolemia.
- Treat the clinical condition or emergency.
- Surgical management if necessary.
- Platelet and factor replacement.

- Heparin therapy (for patients with extensive fibrin deposition and no hemorrhage).

- Administration of activated protein C (for patients with sepsis).

Heparin-Induced Thrombocytopenia

Heparin-induced thrombocytopenia (HIT) affects patients who are exposed to heparin. Type 1 HIT presents within the first two days of heparin therapy and is a non-immune disorder. Type 2 HIT is an immune-mediated condition that occurs four to nine days after heparin exposure. This condition can lead to life-threatening complications as well as loss of limbs.

Diagnosis

- Serotonin release assay (SRA)

- Heparin-induced platelet aggregation assay (HIPA)

- Enzyme-linked immunosorbent assay (ELISA)

- Particle gel immunoassay

Treatment and Management

- Discontinue and avoid all heparin products.

- Administer vitamin K if necessary.

- Administer direct thrombin inhibitors (lepirudin or argatroban).

Anemia

Anemia is a decrease in red blood cells (RBCs), a low quantity of hemoglobin, and/or decreased volume of RBCs. Signs and symptoms of anemia include dyspnea, pallor, tachycardia, weakness, and hypotension. There are numerous causes of anemia, and the condition can be acute or chronic.

- Acute anemia – This usually occurs from blood loss from trauma, GI bleeding, or hemolysis. Extensive loss of blood will alter the hemodynamic status of a patient and requires emergency intervention to stabilize the patient and prevent complications. Treatment involves the rapid infusion of packed RBCs and fresh frozen plasma (FFP).

- Chronic anemia – This form of anemia occurs from conditions such as menorrhagia, hypothyroidism, chronic or acute renal failure, sickle cell disease, and dietary deficiencies. Treatment for chronic anemia is based on the cause of the condition, and usually involves supplementation of iron, transfusion, erythropoietin injections, and surgery.

Allergic and Hypersensitive Reactions

An allergy is sensitivity to some agent or substance, which is known as an allergen. Some allergies are mild whereas others are life-threatening. With a hypersensitive reaction, the degree of exposure, as well as the frequency, can lead to more severe reactions later on. When the first exposure to the allergen occurs, the body releases large amounts of IgE antibodies. However, with repeat exposures, this IgE will trigger histamines and other cytokines to be released. These chemicals can cause serious systemic issues, such as bronchial constriction, pulmonary edema, hypovolemia, and shock.

Allergic and hypersensitive reactions are treated with diphenhydramine, epinephrine, bronchodilators, and steroids. The patient will require hemodynamic support when the reaction causes low blood pressure, altered cardiac contractility, or arrhythmias.

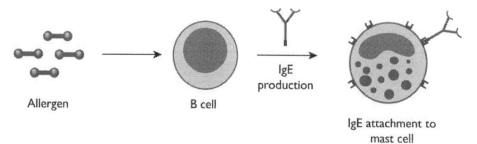

First exposure to allergen

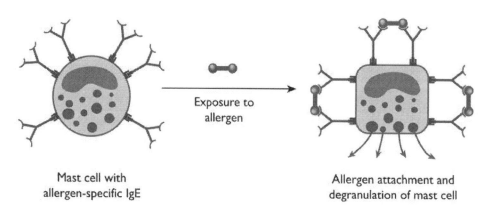

Second exposure to allergen

Human Immunodeficiency Virus and Autoimmune Deficiency Syndrome

Both HIV and AIDS are devastating conditions, but the treatment for these conditions has improved over the last two decades. People with HIV now can live for many years without complications if they follow their medication and lifestyle regimen. If a patient with HIV has a low CD4 T-lymphocyte count, he or she is susceptible to opportunistic infections. The usual treatment for HIV involves antiviral drugs that inhibit the replication of the RNA protein and prevent the virus from entering the body's cells. Also, if the patient has an infection, he or she will receive antibiotics or antifungals, depending on the causative pathogen.

Immunosuppression

Immunosuppression is a deficit in the immunological system that causes a person to have an increased risk for infection. There are several physiological conditions that can cause immunosuppression, and many medications lead to this disorder. Patients who are immunosuppressed are often admitted to the ICU for care.

Patients who have undergone organ transplantation are given immunosuppressant therapy to prevent the rejection of the newly received tissue. These antirejection drugs work on the T and B cells so the donor allograft is not rejected. The CCRN should be aware that patients who are on medications that suppress the immune system must be protected with neutropenic precautions.

Neurology

The nervous system is a complex entity of cells, tissues, structures, and organs. The body uses the nervous system for thinking, making decisions, cognition, behavior, communication, emotion, movement, and sensation. The entire nervous system is made up of two types of cells: neuroglia cells and neurons. Neurotransmitters are chemical substances of the central nervous system that excite, inhibit, or alter the response of another cell. Each neuron releases neurotransmitters.

Anatomy and Physiology

The central nervous system (CNS) includes the brain and spinal cord. This is the command center for the body. The brain receives information and makes decisions. After that, the brain tells the peripheral nervous system (PNS) what to do. The nervous system controls, regulates, and communicates with the various structures, organs, and body parts.

CNS Components

- Cerebrum - Controls memory, thought, and senses.

- Cerebellum - Coordinates movement, balance, and fine motor ability.

- Brain stem - Controls breathing and consciousness.

- Cerebrospinal fluid (CSF) - Clear fluid of the brain and spinal cord that filters contaminants and cushions the CNS.

- Neurons

Primary Cells

- Dendrite (receives nerve signals)

- Cell body (nucleus)

- Axon (carries nerve signals)

- Myelin sheath (around the axon)

Brain

- Brainstem – Consists of the medulla oblongata, pons, and midbrain
- Diencephalon – Consists of the hypothalamus and thalamus
- Cerebellum – Structure that controls voluntary movement and balance
- Cerebrum – Large portion of the brain.
- Lobes: Frontal, parietal, temporal, occipital, and insula

Nerves

- Cranial – 12 pair
- Spinal – 31 pair

PNS Components

The peripheral nervous system includes the structures outside the CNS, such as the nerves. This system sends information to the CNS, and delivers instructions from the CNS. The two divisions of the PNS are:

- Sensory division - Sends information to the CNS.
- Motor division – Receive commands from the CNS.

Autonomic Nervous System

The autonomic nervous system (ANS) is the involuntary portion of the PNS. The two portions of this system are:

- Sympathetic - "Fight or flight" which works in times of stress.
- Parasympathetic - "Feed and breed" which controls rest, reproduction, and digestion.

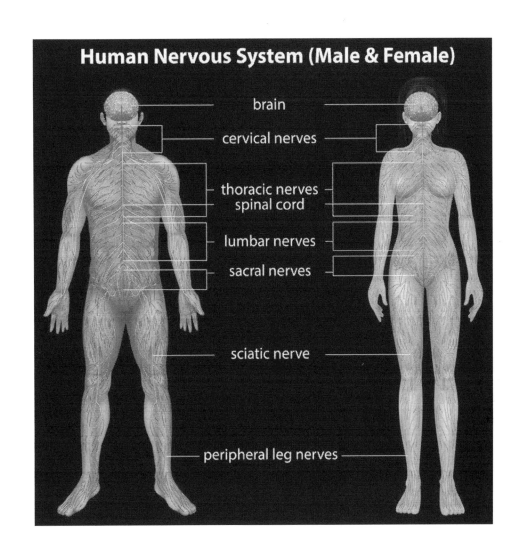

Pathophysiology

Cerebral Aneurysm

A cerebral aneurysm often leads to subarachnoid hemorrhage (SAH), which is a life-threatening condition. Most cerebral aneurysms occur at bifurcations of the larger arteries that are located at the brain's base (circle of Willis).

Signs and Symptoms

- Headache
- Face pain
- Seizures
- Altered level of consciousness
- Autonomic disturbances
- Visual symptoms
- Respiratory distress
- Epistaxis
- Cardiovascular problems
- Nuchal rigidity
- Dilated pupils

Diagnosis

- CBC
- aPTT and PT
- Serum chemistries
- Liver function tests
- ABG
- CT of the head
- MRI of the head

- Angiography

- Transcranial Doppler US

- Echocardiogram

Treatment and Management

- Control of blood pressure

- Prevention of seizures

- Surgery (microsurgical procedures or endovascular coiling)

Brain Death

Brain death is the irreversible loss of brain functions. There are three main criteria for a diagnosis of brain death: coma, absence of brainstem reflexes, and apnea. The diagnosis is made by brain stem reflex assessment and a single apnea test.

Confirmatory Testing

- Angiography – Absence of intracerebral filling at the Circle of Willis or carotid bifurcation.

- MRI angiography – Difficult in the ICU patient due to ventilator hardware and tubing.

- Radionuclide angiography – May not adequately image the posterior fossa vasculature.

- Electroencephalogram – Absence of electrical activity during 30 minutes or more of recording.

- Nuclear brain scan – Absence of uptake of isotope in the brain parenchyma or vasculature.

- Transcranial Doppler US – Small systolic peaks in early systole without diastolic flow, which indicate increased ICP.

Arteriovenous (AV) Malformation

An arteriovenous malformation is a congenital lesion composed of arteries and veins, which are connected by one or more fistulae. AV malformations are often diagnosed in young adults. The shunting of blood leads to atrophy and ischemia in tissues, and arterial blood flow causes venous engorgement, which elevates pressure. When the pressure exerts on the vein wall, rupture occurs.

Signs and Symptoms

- Often silent

- Seizure

- Headaches

- Nausea and vomiting

- Paresis

- Paraplegia

- Decreased level of consciousness

Diagnosis

- CT of the head

- MRI of the head/brain

- Cerebral angiography

Treatment and Management

- Hemodynamic monitoring

- Maintenance of blood pressure within 10 percent of pre-hemorrhage levels

- Anti-seizure medications

- Endovascular embolization

- Surgical resection

- Focal beam radiation

Encephalopathy

- Alcoholic Encephalopathy – This condition occurs when a person drinks excessive alcohol repeatedly and it alters brain activity. The liver develops cirrhosis and ammonia levels directly affect brain tissue. Also, thiamine deficiency causes memory loss, confusion, ataxia, and loss of coordination.

- Anoxic/hypoxic Encephalopathy – This condition occurs when brain tissue is deprived of oxygen, leading to loss of overall brain function. It can occur at any time during a patient's lifespan, such as during cardiac arrest or from prolonged seizures.

- Hypertensive encephalopathy – This condition occurs when elevated blood pressure alters brain function, such as with a hypertensive crisis.

- Infectious encephalopathy – When a patient has encephalitis, from bacteria, virus, or fungi, it can alter the brain tissue and/or the meninges.

- Ischemic encephalopathy – This condition occurs when small blood vessels that take blood to the brain narrow, and there is generalized decreased flow of blood. This causes altered brain function, as with peripheral vascular disease and heart disease.

Hydrocephalus

Hydrocephalus is a disturbance of cerebrospinal fluid (CSF) formation, absorption, and/or flow, which increases CSF volume in the central nervous system (CNS).

Signs and Symptoms

- Altered mentation and cognition

- Headaches

- Neck pain

- Vomiting

- Double and/or blurred vision

- Ataxia and spasticity

- Third ventricle dilation

- Incontinence

Diagnosis

- Head circumference > 98th percentile for age

- Dilated scalp veins

- Tense fontanel

- Increased intracranial pressure (ICP): setting-sun sign, retracted upper lids, and visible sclera above the iris

- Papilledema

- Unsteady gait

- Increased reflexes

Treatment and Management

- Genetic testing and counseling

- Lumbar puncture to evaluate CSF

- Electroencephalography (for patients with seizures)

- CT of the head

- MRI of head/brain

- Surgical treatment with ventriculoperioneal (VP) shunt, ventriculoatrial (VA) shunt, and/or lumboperitoneal shunt.

- Alternatives to shunting, such as opening the stenosed aqueduct, choroid plexectomy, choroid plexus coagulation, or endoscopic fenestration.

Cerebrovascular Accident (CVA)

A cerebrovascular accident (CVA) is also called a stroke, or brain attack. This is the third leading cause of death in the United States. Hemorrhagic stroke occurs when a blood vessel breaks and bleeds into the brain tissue, and these account for around 15 percent of all strokes. Ischemic stroke occurs when a blood clot blocks the blood flow through a blood vessel, resulting in tissue death. These strokes account for 85 percent of all CVAs.

Signs and Symptoms

- Numbness or weakness of face, arm, or leg (unilateral)

- Difficulty speaking

- Trouble understanding others

- Confusion

- Inability to see

- Dizziness

- Loss of balance

- Severe headache

Diagnosis

- Evaluation of level of consciousness, sensation, and function (motor, language, and visual)

- Non-contrast CT of the head/brain

- CBC

- Electrolytes

- Renal function tests

- Coagulation studies

- Liver function tests

Treatment and Management

Treatment involves thrombolytic therapy for ischemic stroke and stopping bleeding for hemorrhagic stroke. Also, complications must be managed, such as hypoglycemia and seizures.

- Thrombolytic therapy (rtPA) – This is given within three hours of symptoms to reduce the long-term effects of a stroke. The usual dose is 0.9 mg/kg for up to 90 mg, with 10 percent to the total dose given as a slow push bolus, and the other 90 percent given over one hour.

- Neurologic checks – Done every 15 to 30 minutes for the first 12 hours.

- Monitoring vital signs and blood glucose.

- Prevention of complications

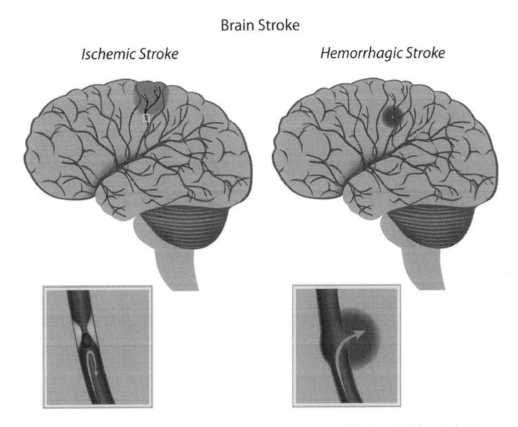

Brain Stroke

Ischemic Stroke   *Hemorrhagic Stroke*

Blockage of blood vessels; lack of blood flow to affected area   Rupture of blood vessels; leakage of blood

Ischemic Stroke

An ischemic stroke occurs when there is a sudden loss of blood flow to a particular brain region, which results in loss of neurologic function. This can occur due to an embolism or thrombotic occlusion of a cerebral artery. Patients who have had a stroke or transient ischemic attack (TIA) should be monitored for diabetes and atrial fibrillation.

Signs and Symptoms

- Hemi-sensory deficits

- Sudden onset of hemiparesis or monoparesis

- Vision loss and deficits

139

- Dysarthria

- Ataxia

- Facial drooping

- Vertigo

- Nystagmus

- Aphasia

- Altered LOC

Diagnosis

- CBC

- Chemistry panel

- Coagulation studies

- Cardiac biomarkers

- Toxicology screen

- CT angiography

- CT perfusion scan

- MRI of head/brain

- Carotid duplex scan

- Digital subtraction angiography

Treatment and Management

- Monitor airway, breathing, and circulation (ABCs)

- Stabilize the patient.

- Correct hypotension or hypertension.

- Correct hypoxia.

- Stabilize glucose level.

- Manage cardiac arrhythmias.

- Initial reperfusion therapy, as ordered.

- Fibrinolytic therapy

- Antiplatelet agents

- Mechanical thrombectomy

Intracranial Hemorrhage

Intracranial hemorrhage is the accumulation of blood within the cranial vault which occurs within the parenchyma of the brain and/or the surrounding meningeal spaces. The meningeal hemorrhage is associated with hematomas and subarachnoid hemorrhage. Intracerebral hemorrhage (ICH) accounts for around 10 percent of all strokes.

Signs and Symptoms

- Altered level of consciousness

- Nausea and vomiting

- Headache

- Seizures

- Prodromal symptoms of focal numbness, weakness, and/or tingling

Diagnosis

- CBC

- aPTT and PT

- Serum chemistries

- Toxicology screen

- Serum alcohol level

- CT of head

- CT angiography – For screening of AVM and vasculitis.

Treatment and Management

- Medical therapy for intracranial hemorrhage is focused on stabilization of the patient and prevention of complications.

- Endotracheal intubation – For patients with poor airway and altered level of consciousness.

- Lower blood pressure and stabilize vital signs.

- IV normotonic fluids – To maintain brain perfusion.

- Correct coagulopathy with vitamin K, fresh frozen plasma, protamine, and/or platelets.

- Anticonvulsants – For patients with seizure activity.

- Surgery to remove large hematomas

- Drain placement into the subdural space to prevent re-accumulation of fluids

Intraventricular Hemorrhage

Intraventricular hemorrhage (IVH) is the presence of blood in the ventricular system of the brain, which can lead to obstructive hydrocephalus. With primary IVH, the blood is in the ventricles, whereas with secondary IVH, the blood in in the parenchymal or subarachnoid areas, as well as the ventricles.

Causes of IVH

- Intraventricular tumors

- Ependymoma

- Choroid plexus

- Intraventricular metastases

- Parenchymal tumors

- Aneurysms

- Arteriovenous malformations

- Sub-ependymal cavernous malformations

- Intracerebral hemorrhage

- Subarachnoid hemorrhage

Signs and Symptoms

- Sudden and severe headache
- Seizures
- Loss of consciousness
- Nausea and vomiting
- Photophobia
- Neck stiffness

Diagnosis

- CT of the head/brain
- MRI of head/brain

Treatment and Management

Treatment involves correcting the underlying cause of hemorrhage and relieving the obstructive hydrocephalus. Serial CTs are required, and the patient often needs a ventricular drain placed to remove fluid (VP shunt).

Neurologic Infectious Disease

Neurological infections occur when microorganisms invade the nervous system.

Signs and Symptoms of Neurological Infection

- Pain
- Edema
- Impaired function
- Confusion
- Drowsiness
- Seizures

Types of Neurological Infections

- Encephalitis – Inflammation of the brain.

- Meningitis – Inflammation of the membranes that cover the brain and spinal cord.

- HIV – Gradually destruction of immune system.

- Other conditions – Includes prion diseases, Lyme disease, tuberculosis, syphilis, and brain abscess.

Neuromuscular Disorders

Neuromuscular disorders affect nerve impulses that control the voluntary muscles, and they typically cause pain and muscle weakness. With certain neuromuscular conditions, the nerves become damaged, and in others, there is compromise of the nerve receptor sites. Most neuromuscular disorders are genetic, but some are the result of an autoimmune issue. These conditions are not curable, but many can be controlled and treated with medications and various therapies.

Muscular Dystrophy

Muscular dystrophy (MD) is a group of 30 or more inherited diseases. These conditions cause loss of muscle and muscle weakness. Many forms of MD appear during infancy or childhood, whereas others do not appear until mid-life or later. The most common types of MD are facioscapulohumeral, Duchenne, Becker, and myotonic. There is no known cure for MD.

Treatment

Treatment for MD is aimed at controlling symptoms, preventing complications, and alleviating pain. This includes:

- Physical therapy
- Speech therapy
- Use of orthopedic devices and appliances for support
- Corrective orthopedic surgery

Medications

- Corticosteroids to slow muscle degeneration
- Immunosuppressant drugs to delay damage to muscle cells
- Anticonvulsants to prevent and control seizure activity
- Antibiotics to treat respiratory infections

Guillain-Barré

Guillain-Barré syndrome causes the patient's immune system to attack his or her PNS. Damage occurs to the nerves, and as a result, the patient's muscles have difficulty responding to the brain. The exact cause of this condition is unknown, but it may be triggered by surgery, infection, or a vaccination.

Signs and Symptoms

- Tingling in the legs (initial symptom)
- Tingling of upper body and extremities
- Paralysis
- Absent reflexes
- Protein in CSF

Diagnosis

The diagnosis of Guillain-Barre syndrome is made based on the patient's symptoms and complaints. However, frequent assessments of negative inspiratory force and vital capacity can help during the initial phase of the disease.

Treatment and Management

- Plasmapheresis
- High-dose immunoglobulin therapy
- Corticosteroids
- Ventilator support
- Physical therapy

Myasthenia Gravis

Myasthenia gravis (MG) is an autoimmune neuromuscular disorder that involves the muscles and the nerves. The patient's body produces antibodies that block muscle cells from receiving neurotransmitters. The antibodies are produced when the patient's immune system considers healthy tissue to be a harmful agent or substance.

Signs and Symptoms

- Weakness of voluntary muscles
- Breathing difficulties (weak chest wall muscles)
- Difficulty talking, lifting, climbing, and rising from a seated position
- Chewing and swallowing problems
- Choking
- Drooling
- Hoarseness
- Double vision
- Eyelid drooping
- Facial paralysis
- Fatigue

Diagnosis

- CT and/or MRI of the chest
- Acetylcholine receptor antibodies
- Nerve conduction studies
- PFT
- EMG
- Edrophonium test

Treatment and Management

There is no known cure for MG, so treatment involves lifestyle changes to help the patient with activities of daily living:

- Frequent rest periods
- Eye patch for double vision
- Avoiding stress
- Avoiding heat exposure
- Ventilator support
- Plasmapheresis – Procedure to remove the plasma that contains antibodies.
- Immunoglobulin infusion – Administer helpful antibodies.
- Thymectomy – Remove thymus that produces antibodies.
- Physical therapy

Medications

- Neostigmine
- Pyridostigmine
- Prednisone
- Azathioprine
- Cyclosporine

Neurosurgery

Neurosurgery is the field of medicine that treats diseases of the brain and spine. The five general categories of neurosurgical conditions are: cerebrovascular, traumatic head injury, degenerative disorders of the spine, CNS tumors, functional conditions, and congenital abnormalities.

Types of Neurosurgical Procedures

- Surgery for congenital abnormalities – This type of surgery is done to correct various congenital conditions.

- Functional neurosurgery – This special procedure is used to manage epilepsy, movement disorders, and pain. It is typically done by placing and fixing a frame on the scalp to stabilize the frame into position and under local anesthesia.

- Epilepsy surgery – This surgery involves a partial anterior temporal lobectomy.

- Deep brain stimulation – This procedure involves implantation of electrodes into the area of the brain that affects mood. Electrical impulses are transmitted through these electrodes to relieve depression and other mood disturbances.

- Neuro-endoscopy – This procedure is a minimally invasive treatment for deep seated brain tumors and masses of the skull base. A small fiber optic lens is used to visualize the tumor(s) that lie within the ventricular system of the brain, and biopsy is done during this.

- Stereotactic neurosurgery – This procedure involves 3D imaging to locate and treat various targets of the nervous system.

- Craniotomy – This is a procedure in which a skull bone flap is removed so the surgeon can reach the tumor.

- Craniectomy – This procedure involves excision of a portion of the skull, which is not replaced. It is often done for decompression after cerebral de-bulking or to remove bone fragments following a skull fracture.

- Cranioplasty – This surgery is done to repair the skull with synthetic materials. The surgeon will drill Burr holes in the skull to access the structures. This procedure is done to evacuate subdural or epidural hematomas, to insert an ICP-monitoring device, or to insert an intraventricular catheter.

Seizure Disorders

Seizures occur because of sudden, abnormal electrical activity of the brain. Focal (partial) seizures occur in only one portion of the brain, whereas generalized seizures occur from abnormal activity of both sides of the brain. Most seizures only last 1 to 3 minutes and do not result in harm. However, some seizures persist for longer than 5 minutes.

Epilepsy is a brain disorder that is characterized by recurring seizures from a neurobiological, psychological, cognitive, and/or social condition. Seizures can be caused from high fevers, medications, head injuries, and certain diseases and disorders. Also, uremia, hypoglycemia, electrolyte disturbances, and acid-base imbalances can cause seizures in patients with brain injury, stroke, or those who have had recent cranial surgery.

Seizure Phases

- Prodromal phase – This is the activity and signs that occur before seizure, such as headache and depressed mood.

- Aural phase – During this phase, there is a sensation that can be visual, auditory, visceral, or gustatory in nature (aura).

- Ictal phase – This is the actual seizure activity when the patient is unconscious and unresponsive.

- Post-ictal phase – This occurs immediately after seizure activity, and during this stage, the patient will be disoriented, drowsy, confused, and have no memory of what happened.

Signs and Symptoms

- Automatisms – Coordinated, involuntary motor activities, such as chewing, pacing, lip smacking, and fidgeting.

- Clonus – Pattern of spasm that occurs with muscle rigidity and is followed by muscle relaxation.

- Autonomic – These symptoms occur in response to some form of autonomic nervous system stimulation, such as sweating, pallor, flushing, and pupil dilation.

Types of Seizures

- Absence – These seizures occur during childhood and often appear in clusters (dozens or hundreds of times per day). They only last 5 to 10 seconds.

- Atypical Absence – These usually begin before the age of five years and are associated with mental retardation. They last longer than absence seizures, and the patient will have muscle spasms.

- Myoclonic – These are characterized by brief and sudden arm muscle contractions, and the patient does not lose consciousness.

- Clonic – These are characterized by rhythmic, repetitive movements of the face, neck, and arms, with movement being symmetric and bilateral.

- Tonic-clonic – Also called grand mal, these are the most common generalized seizures, and they can lead to tongue biting, limb fractures, and head trauma. The patient will have violent shaking and muscle contractions with tonic-clonic activity.

- Atonic – These seizures involve sudden loss of muscle control, so the patient will often fall to the floor or out of the chair.

- Partial – These seizures do not alter consciousness, and the symptoms depend on the region of the brain that is involved.

- Simple Partial – With this activity, the patient is alert and can have sensory, motor, autonomic, and/or cognitive deficits.

- Complex Partial – These are the most common type of epileptic seizures. The patient will lose consciousness and automatisms may occur.

Diagnosis

Diagnosing seizure disorders requires testing and assessing the patient's clinical history. Tests include:

- Prolactin levels – Obtain shortly after the seizure to evaluate etiology and seizure type.

- CSF examination – Evaluate for meningitis and encephalitis.

- EEG

- MRI or CT of head/brain

Treatment and Management

- Preventing injury
- Maintaining the airway
- Intubation if necessary
- Oxygen supplementation
- Lorazepam or diazepam to stop activity
- Anticonvulsants to prevent activity
- Vagal nerve stimulator therapy
- Lobectomy
- Lesionectomy

Medication Therapy

- Sodium channel blockers: phenytoin, carbamazepine, lamotrigine, oxcarbazepine, and topiramate.
- Slow inactivation of sodium channel: lacosamide and rufinamide.
- Gamma aminobutyric acid A receptor enhancers: phenobarbital and benzodiazepines.
- NMDA receptor blockers: felbamate
- AMPA receptor blockers: perampanel
- T-calcium channel blockers: valproate and ethosuximide
- H-current modulators: gabapentin and lamotrigine
- N- and L-calcium channel blockers: topiramate, lamotrigine, zonisamide, and valproate.
- Carbonic anhydrase inhibitors: zonisamide and topiramate

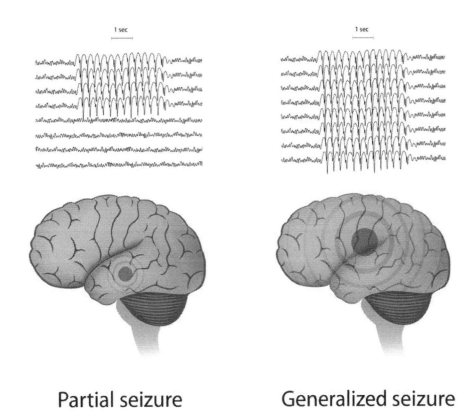

Partial seizure   Generalized seizure

Space-Occupying Brain Lesions

A space-occupying brain lesion is often related to malignant cancer, but it can also be caused by a hematoma or abscess. Approximately 50 percent of intracerebral tumors are primary, but the other 50 percent originate outside the CNS and metastasize to the brain. In adults, the majority of brain tumors are from gliomas, meningiomas, acoustic neuromas, pituitary adenomas, or metastases. Primary cerebral lesions include glioblastoma multiform, astrocytoma, oligodendrogliomas, and ependymoas. The most common primary site of cancer is lung cancer, followed by breast, colon, and melanoma.

Signs and Symptoms

The signs and symptom of a brain lesion vary, but there are usually general characteristics. These include:

- Behavioral changes

155

- Elevated intracranial pressure

- Seizures

- Hydrocephalus

- Stroke-like symptoms

- Headache

- Papilledema

- Nausea and vomiting

- Syncope

- Weakness and gait disturbance

- Deficits in vision and speech

Signs and Symptoms by Lesion Site

- Cerebellum – Space-occupying lesions in this area can cause nystagmus, intention tremor, staccato speech, and truncal ataxia. Causes include stroke, multiple sclerosis, hemangioma, acoustic neuroma, abscess, and chronic alcohol use.

- Temporal lobe – These lesions can cause emotional changes, behavioral disturbances, depersonalization, dysphasia, visual field defects, forgetfulness, and functional psychosis.

- Frontal lobe – These tumors can cause anosmia, dysphasia, personality changes, and hemiparesis.

- Parietal lobe – These lesions can cause decreased two-point discrimination, asterognosis, hemi-sensory loss, dysphagia, sensory inattention, and left-right disorientation.

- Occipital lobe – These tumors cause visual defects. Causes include pituitary adenoma, lesion of the optic chiasm, and optic tract lesion.

- Corpus callosum – Lesions in this region cause rapid intellectual deterioration, with loss of communication between the two lobes.

- Midbrain – Tumors of the midbrain cause unequal pupils, somnolence, amnesia, and inability to move the eyes up or down.

- Pituitary tumors – These lesions cause homonymous hemianopia and endocrine effects.

Diagnosis

- CBC

- Liver function tests

- Electrolytes

- Skull x-ray

- CT and/or MRI of head/brain

- Biopsy of lesion

- Chest x-ray and mammogram (if primary tumor suspected)

Treatment and Management

The primary goals for the CCRN in the care of the patient with a space-occupying brain lesion are to monitor intracranial pressure and stabilize, prevent complications, and offer symptomatic therapy. This includes the use of anticonvulsants for seizure control and prevention, as well as analgesics for headaches and antiemetic for nausea and/or vomiting.

Gastrointestinal

The gastrointestinal (GI) system is composed of the tubular structures that extend from the mouth to the anus, as well as the accessory organs of digestion. The GI system breaks down ingested food, gives the body nutrition, and eliminates waste.

Anatomy and Physiology

The abdominal cavity is separated from the thoracic cavity by the diaphragm. It is divided into four quadrants: left upper quadrant (LUQ), left lower quadrant (LLQ), right upper quadrant (RUQ), and right lower quadrant (RLQ). The abdominal organs are:

- Esophagus - Tube that runs from mouth to stomach and lies behind the trachea.

- Stomach - Digestive organ in the LUQ and receives and breaks down food.

- Pancreas - An organ of the RUQ that aids in digestion, produces insulin, and regulates blood sugar.

- Liver - A solid organ in the RUQ that helps filter toxins, break down fat, and produce cholesterol.

- Gallbladder - A small hollow RUQ organ that lies beneath the liver, stores bile, and releases bile during digestion.

- Appendix - A RLQ small organ that is often obstructed, leading to inflammation, infection, and/or rupture.

- Spleen - A small solid LUQ organ that filters blood.

- Kidneys - Two solid organs that are positioned in the mid-abdomen to control fluid, filter waste, and regulate pH balance.

- Small intestine - A hollow tubular organ in both lower quadrants that digests fat and releases enzymes.

- Large intestine - A hollow organ of the lower abdomen that pulls out liquid and forms solid stool.

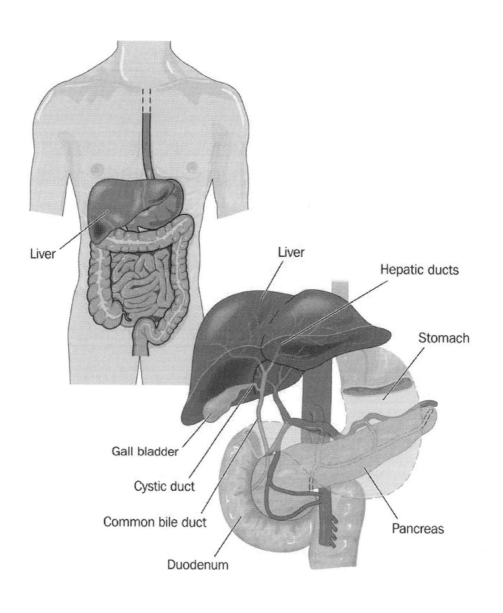

Liver

Liver

Hepatic ducts

Stomach

Gall bladder

Cystic duct

Common bile duct

Pancreas

Duodenum

Pathophysiology

Acute Abdominal Trauma

Acute abdominal trauma is a leading cause of morbidity and mortality for all ages. This injury can occur secondary to motor vehicle or other accidents.

Signs and Symptoms

- Abdominal pain
- Abdominal tenderness
- GI hemorrhage
- Hypovolemia
- Peritoneal irritation
- Lap belt marks
- Ecchymosis of the flanks (Grey Turner sign)
- Ecchymosis of the umbilicus (Cullen sign)
- Abdominal distention
- Abnormal bowel sounds
- Abdominal bruit
- Guarding, rigidity, and/or rebound tenderness

Diagnosis

- Diagnostic peritoneal lavage (DPL)
- Focused Assessment with Sonography for Trauma (FAST)
- Abdominal x-rays
- CT of the abdomen

Treatment and Management

- Laparotomy for patients with signs of peritonitis, shock, hemorrhage, or hemoperitoneum findings on DPL or FAST.

- Splenic artery embolotherapy for blunt spleen injury.

- Laparoscopy to explore if necessary.

- Splenectomy or nephrectomy to remove organ as necessary.

- Anastomosis to join bowel sections if separated.

- Monitor vital signs.

- Administer supplemental oxygen as necessary.

- Anti-thrombotic stockings to prevent DVT.

Acute GI Hemorrhage

GI hemorrhage is any bleeding that originates along the GI tract, from mouth to anus. Upper GI hemorrhage includes the esophagus, stomach, and upper portion of the small intestine. Lower GI bleeding involves the small intestine, colon, and anus.

Signs and Symptoms

- Vomiting blood

- Passing large amounts of bright red blood from the rectum

- Dark, tarry stools

- Bloody stools

- Hematemesis

- Abdominal pain

- Epigastric pain

- Weakness

- Fatigue

- Syncope

- Weight loss

- Jaundice

Causes of GI Hemorrhage

- Hemorrhoids

- Colon cancer

- Cancer of the esophagus, stomach, or small intestine

- Intestinal polyps

- Diverticular rupture

- Crohn's disease

- Ulcerative colitis

- Esophageal varices

- Gastric or peptic ulcer

- Injury of the bowel

Diagnosis

- Occult stool evaluation

- CBC

- Electrolytes

- Anticoagulation studies

- Bleeding time

- Sigmoidoscopy

- Colonoscopy

- Esophagogastroduodenoscopy (EGD)

- Abdominal CT scan

- Abdominal MRI scan

- Angiography

- Type and cross blood

Treatment and Management

- IV fluid administration

- Blood transfusions

- Gastric lavage

- Urinary catheter

- Surgical repair if necessary

- High-dose IV proton pump inhibitors for patients with peptic ulcer

Intestinal Ischemia and Infarction

Intestinal ischemia occurs when there is damage to a part of the intestine, and infarction results from decreased blood supply. These conditions are caused by hernia, adhesions, embolus, thrombosis, and low blood pressure.

Signs and Symptoms

- Abdominal pain

- Fever

- Diarrhea

- Nausea and vomiting

Diagnosis

- CBC

- Angiogram

- CT scan of the abdomen

- Abdominal US

Treatment and Management

- Surgery to remove the infarcted section of intestine and reconnect the remaining ends. For some patients, a colostomy and/or ileostomy is necessary.

- Provide ordered IV fluids.

- Monitor vital signs.

- Administer medications as ordered.

Small Bowel Obstruction

A small bowel obstruction (SBO) is caused by postoperative adhesions in 60 percent of cases, with malignancy, hernias, and Crohn's disease causing the other 40 percent. SBO is characterized as either partial or complete and can be simple or strangulated.

Signs and Symptoms

- Intermittent abdominal pain (simple obstruction)

- Abdominal cramping

- Abdominal distention

- Nausea and vomiting (proximal obstructions)

- Diarrhea

- Fever

- Tachycardia

Diagnosis

- CBC

- BUN and creatinine

- Serum chemistries

- Lactate dehydrogenase tests

- UA

- Type and cross match blood

- Phosphate level

- Liver function studies

- Abdominal x-rays

- Enteroclysis

- CT of the abdomen

- US of the abdomen

Treatment and Management

- Inflammatory Bowel Disease (IBD) – High-dose steroids, bowel rest, and surgical treatment with bowel resection and/or strictureplasty

- Malignant Tumor – Surgical resection when feasible.

- Intra-abdominal Abscess – CT scan-guided drainage.

- Radiation Enteritis – IV corticosteroids and supportive care.

- Adhesions – Surgery to remove.

- Strangulated Obstruction – Medical emergency and requires laparoscopy.

GI Surgeries and Procedures

Colonoscopy

The colonoscopy is done with a long, thin, flexible scope that has a light and a small camera at the end. The physician inserts the scope and takes pictures of the colon to assess for suspicious growths and masses. During a colonoscopy, the doctor may remove polyps and take biopsies for colorectal cancer screening. Also, this 30 minute procedure is done to evaluate changes in bowel habits, bleeding, and abdominal pain. Most patients are kept comfortable with IV sedation.

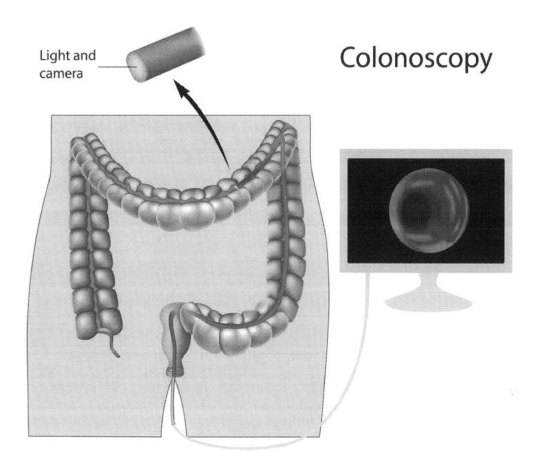

Colonoscopy

Light and camera

Endoscopic Retrograde Cholangiopancreatography (ERCP)

The endoscopic retrograde cholangiopancreatography (ERCP) procedure is done with an endoscope inserted through the esophagus, stomach and the first portion of the small intestine. When the scope reaches the common bile duct, the physician injects dye and takes x-rays. The ERCP is done to evaluate abdominal pain, gallstones, tumors, scar tissue, and jaundice. IV sedation is given and the patient remains semi-conscious during the procedure, which takes 30 to 45 minutes.

Endoscopic Ultrasound (EUS)

The endoscopic ultrasound (EUS) is used to assess and evaluate the upper and lower gastrointestinal tract. The physician uses and endoscope that emits sound waves to create visual images of the GI tract. EUS is used to assess tumors or detect diseases of the bile duct, gallbladder, and/or pancreas. The patient receives IV sedation during this 45-minute procedure.

Flexible Sigmoidoscopy

A sigmoidoscopy is a procedure to examine the inside of the sigmoid colon (large bowel). This is often done to assess blood loss, abdominal pain, and changes in bowel habits, and the procedure takes around 15 minutes.

Liver Biopsy

A liver biopsy is done to determine fibrosis and inflammation of the liver and to diagnoses various diseases. The patient is given a local anesthetic, and the physician uses a long, narrow needle to obtain a small piece of liver tissue.

Upper GI Endoscopy

An upper GI endoscopy is done to examine the upper GI tract with an endoscope. The physician will do this procedure to evaluate and diagnose problems such as difficulty swallowing, heartburn, abdominal pain, bleeding, tumors, and ulcerations. IV sedation is given for this 15 minute procedure.

Double Balloon Enteroscopy

A double balloon enteroscopy is a method of evaluating the small intestine, and it involves the use of a high-resolution video that has a latex balloon attached to the tip of the device. This is inflated and deflated as needed for assessment of GI bleeding, unexplained diarrhea, Crohn's disease, and pancreatobiliary disease.

Gastric Surgeries

- Total gastrectomy – Complete removal of the stomach and esophageal-jejunal anastomosis.

- Subtotal or partial gastrectomy – Partial removal of the stomach.

- Gastrostomy – Creation of a rectangular stomach flap for a stoma to be used for intermittent tube feedings.

Hernia Surgeries

- Hernioplasty – Reconstructive hernia repair.

- Herniorrhaphy – Surgical repair of a hernia.

Bowel Surgeries

- Appendectomy – Removal of the appendix.

- Bowel resection – Excision of a segment of the small or large bowel.

- Cholecystectomy – Removal of the gallbladder.

Cirrhosis

Cirrhosis is a diffuse hepatic process characterized by abnormal liver nodules and fibrosis. The majority of cases of cirrhosis are due to chronic alcohol consumption, but the progression of liver injury to cirrhosis can occur in just a few weeks.

Signs and Symptoms

Most of the signs and symptoms of cirrhosis stem from a decrease in hepatic synthetic function, portal hypertension, and a decrease in liver detoxification ability:

- Portal hypertension

- Hepatomegaly

- Abdominal pain

- Ascites

- Bulging flanks

- Hepatic encephalopathy

- Fatigue

- Anorexia

- Weight loss

- Muscle wasting

- Jaundice

- Spider angioma

- Telangiectasia

- Finger clubbing

Diagnosis

- Liver function tests

- Creatinine clearance

- Urine osmolality

- Angiogram

- Electroencephalography

- CT of the head/brain

- Paracentesis

- Liver biopsy

Treatment and Management

- Phlebotomy for hemochromatosis

- Prednisone and azathioprine for autoimmune hepatitis

- Interferon and antiviral agents for hepatitis of viral origin

- Trientine and zinc for Wilson disease

- Diuretics, paracentesis, and shuts for ascites

- Liver transplantation

Portal Hypertension

Portal hypertension is usually caused by cirrhosis. Two factors that lead to the development of portal hypertension are vascular resistance and altered blood flow.

Signs and Symptoms

- Weakness and malaise
- Weight loss
- Anorexia
- Jaundice
- Ascites
- Splenomegaly
- Spider angioma
- Gynecomastia and testicular atrophy in males
- Pruritus
- Bruising and bleeding
- Muscle cramps
- Palmar erythema
- Arterial hypotension

Diagnosis

- CBC
- Liver function tests
- Type and cross match blood
- aPTT and PT
- BUN and creatinine
- Electrolytes
- Albumin levels
- Antibody testing
- Abdomen and liver duplex Doppler US
- CT scan
- MRI scan
- Angiography when bleeding occurs

- Liver biopsy

- Histology evaluation

- Upper GI endoscopy

Treatment and Management

- Maintain airway

- Evaluate circulation

- NG tube placement

- Portal pressure reduction with an anti-secretory agent by IV infusion

- Replace volume loss

- Control and prevent bleeding of esophageal varices

- Administer vasoconstrictors (octreotide or vasopressin) and beta-blockers

- Endoscopic variceal ligation (EVL)

- Balloon-tube tamponade

- Transjugular intrahepatic portosystemic shunt (TIPS)

Esophageal Varices

Esophageal varices are enlarged veins that often bleed. They are caused by cirrhosis when scarring obscures the flow of blood through the liver, and more blood must flow through the esophageal veins. With the extra blood, the veins balloon outward, and heavy bleeding occurs.

Signs and Symptoms

- Black, tarry stools

- Blood stools

- Pallor

- Dizziness

- Nausea and vomiting

- Vomiting blood

- Tachycardia

- Hypotension

Diagnosis

- Occult blood

- CBC

- Coagulation studies

- Electrolytes

- Liver function tests

- EGD

Treatment and Management

The goal of esophageal varices treatment is to stop acute bleeding and prevent complications (shock and death). To stop the bleeding, healthcare providers perform endoscopy to inject the varices with clotting medication or use rubber band ligation. Once the bleeding has stopped, the varices are treated with beta blockers and the TIPS procedure to decrease pressure in the veins.

Esophageal Varices

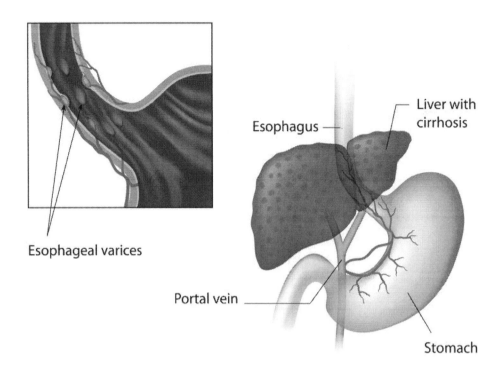

Esophageal varices

Esophagus

Liver with cirrhosis

Portal vein

Stomach

Hepatic Failure

Acute liver failure (hepatic failure) occurs when there is rapid deterioration of liver function that results in coagulopathy. This condition often affects young people and has a high mortality rate.

Signs and Symptoms

- Encephalopathy

- Cerebral edema

- Hypertension and/or bradycardia

- Ascites

- Abdominal pain

- Hematemesis

- Black, tarry stools

Diagnosis

- Prothrombin time with INR
- CBC
- Liver function tests
- Bilirubin level
- Glucose level
- Arterial lactate level
- BUN and creatinine
- Drug screening for patients with a history of substance use/abuse
- Acetaminophen levels
- Blood cultures for patients with possible infection
- Viral serology for various hepatitis viruses, herpes simplex virus, and cytomegalovirus
- EEG
- Intracranial pressure monitoring
- Hepatic Doppler US
- Abdominal CT scan
- MRI of the abdomen
- Cranial CT scan
- Liver biopsy

Treatment and Management

- Protection of airway
- Fluid management
- Monitoring vital signs
- Administer antidotes (silibinin, charcoal, and N-acetylcysteine)
- Diuretics
- Barbiturate agents

- Benzodiazepines
- Liver transplantation

Hepatic Coma

Hepatic coma, also called hepatic encephalopathy, is the loss of brain function related to inability of the liver to remove blood toxins. It is caused by cirrhosis, hepatitis, and conditions that alter blood circulation of the liver. Ammonia is produced by the body when proteins are digested and broken down, and if the liver cannot remove this substance, it accumulates in the bloodstream.

Triggers for Hepatic Coma/Encephalopathy

- Dehydration
- Excessive consumption of protein
- Electrolyte imbalances
- GI bleeding
- Renal insufficiency
- Hypoxemia
- Surgery
- CNS depressant medications, such as benzodiazepines and barbiturates

Signs and Symptoms

- Musty or sweet breath odor
- Confusion
- Memory difficulties
- Poor concentration
- Mental fogginess
- Poor judgment
- Trouble with fine motor ability

- Hand tremor
- Slurred speech
- Slow or sluggish movement

Diagnosis
- CBC
- Liver function test
- Ammonia level
- Electrolytes
- BUN and creatinine
- EEG
- CT of head/brain
- MRI of head/brain

Treatment and Management
- Stop GI bleeding
- Correct electrolyte imbalances
- Monitor vital signs
- Administer IV fluids
- Correct malnutrition
- Lactulose to prevent ammonia formation in the intestines
- Rifaximin to treat intestinal bacteria

Pancreatitis

Acute pancreatitis is inflammation of the pancreas that affects men more often than women. The pancreas produces enzymes and the hormones glucagon and insulin. When the enzymes become active inside the pancreas, they can cause bleeding, swelling and damage the pancreatic tissue and blood vessels, which is called pancreatitis. More than 70 percent of cases of acute pancreatitis are associated with alcohol abuse, but the condition is also linked to blockage of the pancreatic duct, trauma, and autoimmune conditions.

Signs and Symptoms

- Abdominal pain that is boring, steady, and dull
- Nausea and vomiting
- Anorexia
- Diarrhea
- Fever
- Abdominal guarding
- Abdominal distention
- Cullen sign
- Grey-Turner sign

Diagnosis

- Liver function tests
- Serum amylase and lipase
- BUN and creatinine
- Electrolytes
- Serum glucose
- CBC
- C-reactive protein (CRP)
- ABG
- Serum lactic dehydrogenase (LDH) and bicarbonate levels
- Abdominal x-rays
- Abdominal US
- EUS

- Abdominal CT scan

- ERCP

- Magnetic resonance cholangiopancreatography (MRCP)

Treatment and Management

- IV fluids and nutritional support

- Antibiotic therapy and prophylaxis

- Surgical intervention when complication is present

- Cholecystectomy for removal of gallstone

- Placement of drain tube for pancreatic duct obstruction and disruption

- Image-guided aspiration for infected pancreatic necrosis

- Percutaneous catheter drainage for abscess

- Surgical debridement for abscess

Renal

The renal system is a complex filtering body system responsible for homeostasis, maintain acid-base balance and excreting wastes. The urinary collection system is composed of the ureters, bladder, and urethra.

Anatomy and Physiology

The renal and urinary system controls fluid balance and filters waste from the blood via the kidneys. The ureters are two tubes that connect each kidney to the bladder. Urine moves from the kidneys, through the ureters, and then down the urethra to exit the body. This system works with the reproductive system to remove metabolic waste materials from the body, such as uric acid, urea, nitrogenous waste, and creatinine. The urinary system also maintains electrolyte balance and assists the liver in body detoxification.

Anatomy

- Kidneys - Two organs that control pH balance (acid/base), secrete berenin, vitamin D, and erythropoietin, and stimulate red blood cell production.

- Cortex - Outer layer of the kidney.

- Medullar - Inner portion of the kidney.

- Hilum - Middle section of the kidney.

- Papilla - Inner part of the pyramids.

- Nephrons - Operational units of the kidneys.

- Ureters - Narrow tubules that transport urine from the kidneys to the bladder.

- Urinary Bladder - Sac-like reservoir for the urine.

- Urethra - Tube that transport urine from the bladder to outside the body.

Basic steps in urine formation

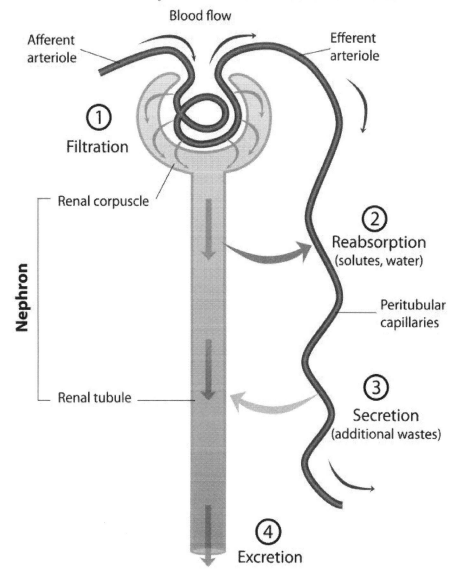

The Acute Dialysis Quality Initiative (ADQI) RIFLE Classification

- Risk – Increase in creatinine level X 1.5, a decrease in GFR by 25%, or UO of <0.5 mL/kg/hr for 6 hours.

- Injury – Increase in creatinine level X 2.0, decrease in GFR by 50%, or UO <0.5 mL/kg/h for 12 hours.

- Failure – Increase in creatinine level X 3.0, decrease in GFR by 75%, creatinine level > 4mg/dL with increase of >0.5 mg/dL, UO < 0.3 mL/kg/h for 24 hours, or anuria for 12 hours.

- Loss – Persistent ARF with complete loss of kidney function for more than four weeks.

- End-stage kidney disease – Kidney function loss for greater than three months.

Pathophysiology

Acute Renal Failure

Acute renal failure (ARF) occurs in around five percent of hospitalized patients, and the etiology can be pre-renal, intrinsic, or post-renal. The majority of cases are pre-renal or related to acute tubular necrosis, which is an intrinsic condition caused by toxins or ischemia. In ARF, the glomerular filtration rate (GFR) decreases, the excretion of nitrogenous waste is greatly reduced, and electrolyte and fluid balance cannot be maintained.

Diagnosis

- Creatinine

- BUN

- GFR

- Microscopic urinalysis

- Cystatin C

- CBC

- Chemistry studies

- Renal US

- Chest x-ray

- ECG

Calculating GFR

Modification of Diet in Renal Disease (MDRD) equation: GFR, in mL/min per 1.73 mm^2 = 186.3 X ((Serum Creatinine) exp[-1.154]) X (Age exp[-0.203]) X (0.742 if female) X (1.21 if African American)

Treatment and Management

Patients with ARF have difficulty with fluid management, and hypovolemia will potentiate and exacerbate the condition. To adequately manage this condition, the CCRN should do the following:

- Invasive hemodynamic monitoring

- Urinary catheter placement

- Renal replacement therapy (RRT) by intermittent hemodialysis (IHD), peritoneal dialysis (PD), or continuous venovenous hemodiafiltration (CVVHD).

- Medications, such as diuretics and vasodilators.

Acute Tubular Necrosis (ATN)

Acute tubular necrosis (ATN) is considered intra-renal, with 75 percent of cases being of this type. The majority of hospital-acquired renal failure is ATN, which occurs from damage to the renal tubular epithelium from nephrotoxins or injury. When there is serious hypoperfusion to the kidneys, the tubular cell membranes become damaged and protein casts form, which obstruct the renal tubules. With obstruction and ischemia, there is reduced blood and fluid flow to the kidneys, and the afferent and efferent arterioles cannot regulate as they should. Ischemic ATN occurs from burns, hemorrhage, sepsis, MI, PE, and placenta previa. Drugs known to damage the kidneys include bacterial endotoxins and chemical agents.

Four Phases of ATN

- Onset phase (few hours to several days) –ATN first starts and is difficult to detect. GFR is reduced at this time due to low pressure and hypoperfusion.

- Oliguric/anuric phase (5 to 8 days) – Common with ischemic ATN; kidney damage occurs during this phase.

- Diuretic phase (several weeks) – The patient experiences polyuria and output of urine around 3 to 4 L/day. Tubular function is slow to return and hypovolemia can occur.

- Recovery stage (up to two years) – Tubular function returns to normal stage, and 33 percent of patients are left with some renal insufficiency.

Chronic Renal Failure

Chronic renal failure (CRF), also known as chronic kidney disease (CKD), is the slow loss of renal function over time. The final stage of CRF is end-stage renal disease (ESRD), where the kidneys can no longer remove waste and fluid from the body and dialysis is required.

Causes of CRF

- Diabetes
- High blood pressure
- Autoimmune disorders
- Polycystic kidney disease
- Renal trauma or injury
- Toxins and chemicals
- Reflux nephropathy
- Certain medications and chemotherapies
- Renal calculi
- Kidney infection

Signs and Symptoms

- Fatigue and malaise
- Loss of appetite
- Loss of weight
- Headaches
- Pruritus and dry skin
- Nausea and vomiting
- Abnormal skin color
- Breath odor
- Muscle cramps and pain

- Drowsiness

- Concentration difficulties

- Bruising

- Swelling and numbness of the hands and/or feet

- Excessive thirst

Diagnosis

- Urinalysis

- Creatinine

- BUN

- Creatinine clearance

- Chemistry studies

- CBC

- CT of the abdomen

- MRI of the abdomen

- US of the abdomen

- Renal scan

- Renal biopsy

Treatment and Management

- Control Blood Pressure – May be prescribed an ACE inhibitor or ARB

- Diet – Eat low fat, low sodium, and low protein diet

- Glucose Control - Diet and medications to keep blood sugar stable

- Phosphate Binders – Medicines to prevent high phosphorus levels

- Supplements – Take calcium, iron, and vitamin D as prescribed

- Fluid Restriction – The physician will set an amount of daily fluid intake

Electrolyte Imbalances

Electrolytes (ions) are charged particles in body fluids that transmit impulses for muscle, nerve, and heart function. Positive ions are cations, whereas negative ones are anions. The balance of cations and anions should be equal; if not, the patient is at risk for a life-threatening condition. The most common causes of electrolyte imbalance is dehydration, renal dysfunction, diabetic ketoacidosis, and head injury.

Hypernatremia

Sodium (Na) is a cation in the extracellular fluid that maintains osmolality. Hypernatremia occurs when either too much water is lost or too much salt is ingested or received into the body. Older adults are at risk for hypernatremia following fever or surgery due to volume depletion and a diminished thirst mechanism. Also, patients on diuretic therapy or fluid restrictions are at risk for hypernatremia.

Signs and Symptoms

- Disorientation
- Irritability
- Weakness
- Muscle twitching
- Low urine output

Treatment and Management

- Correcting the underlying cause.
- Replacing volume orally.
- Administering IV of isotonic solutions.
- Monitoring serum sodium and osmolality.
- Monitoring intake and output.

Hyponatremia

Hyponatremia occurs when the patient loses more sodium than water or when excessive fluid intake dilutes the body's sodium concentration. This can be caused from HF, SIADH, diarrhea, diuretics, suctioning, or laxative use. Severe hyponatremia can cause permanent neurological damage if the sodium falls below 110 mEq/L.

Signs and Symptoms

- Hypotension

- Palpitations

- Tachycardia

- Confusion

- Lethargy

- Nausea and/or vomiting

Treatment and Management

- Correcting the underlying cause.

- Replacing sodium through IV fluids or oral intake.

- For severe hyponatremia, rapid infusion of serum sodium (hypertonic 3% NaCl).

Hyperkalemia

Potassium (K) is a major intracellular cation important for cardiac, nerve, and muscle function. Elevated potassium will stimulate the release of aldosterone, which triggers sodium retention. The most common cause of hyperkalemia is renal disease, acidosis, sodium depletion, aldosterone deficiency, and excessive potassium supplements.

Signs and Symptoms

- ECG changes (peaked T waves, prolonged PR interval, and wide QRS complex)

- Muscle weakness

- Fatigue

- Lethargy

- Abdominal cramping

- Cardiac arrest

Treatment and Management

- IV diuretics

- Sodium polystyrene suflonate (Kayexalate)

- For severe hyperkalemia, IV calcium chloride or calcium gluconate

Hypokalemia

The most common cause of hypokalemia is inadequate potassium supplementation in diuretic therapy, as well as nasogastric suctioning and diarrhea. With acidosis, the pH returns to normal, and potassium enters the cells. This can lower the serum potassium and put the patient at risk for hypokalemia.

Signs and Symptoms

- Drowsiness

- Fatigue

- Muscle weakness

- Leg cramps

- Confusion

- Loss of appetite

- Abdominal distention

- ECG changes (inverted T waves, depressed ST segment, PATs, and PVCs)

Treatment and Management

- Replacing potassium IV, running 20 mEqs in 100 mL over 60 minutes.

- Monitor ECG.

- Monitor urine output.

Hypermagnesemia

Magnesium is a cation in the cells that helps with energy production, muscle function, and carbohydrate and protein metabolism. The main cause of this electrolyte imbalance is renal failure, but other causes include use of antacids and laxatives, as well as diabetic ketoacidosis.

Signs and Symptoms

- Lethargy

- Altered mental status

- Respiratory depression

- Muscle weakness

- Impaired cardiac conduction and contractility

- Bradycardia

- Hypotension

- ECG changes (prolonged PR interval, wide QRS complex, or prolonged QT interval)

Treatment and Management

- Diuretic therapy to promote magnesium loss.

- IV calcium gluconate IV to improve cardiac function.

- Hemodialysis for severe hypermagnesemia and renal failure.

Hypomagnesemia

Low magnesium increases cardiac muscle irritability. Hypomagnesemia can produce life-threatening dysrhythmias, particularly for patients who have had a recent MI.

Signs and Symptoms

- Lethargy

- Confusion

- Coma

- ECG (flat or inverted T wave, short AT interval, and ST segment depression)

Treatment and Management

- IV or oral magnesium therapy

- Monitoring ECG

Acid-Base Balance

Chloride (Cl) and bicarbonate (HCO3) are two main extracellular anions. They maintain acid-base balance in the body. The ration between acids and bases is numerically expressed as pH, with normal pH being 7.35 to 7.45. A rise in pH is alkalosis and a low pH is acidosis. With too little Cl, HCO3 accumulates and metabolic alkalosis occurs. Too much Cl causes acidosis and dehydration.

Causes of Hypochloremia

- Vomiting

- Nasogastric suctioning

- Diuretics

Causes of Elevated Bicarbonate

- Antacids

- IV fluids

- Massive blood transfusions

Multisystem

Multisystem and Multi-Organ Conditions

The multisystem section covers many conditions that affect more than one body system at a time. Multi-organ conditions make patient care complex, increase a patient's length of stay in the ICU, boost care provision costs, and increase morbidity and mortality rates.

Asphyxia

Asphyxia (asphyxiation) is a deficient supply of oxygen to the body that occurs from abnormal breathing and oxygen supply, which leads to generalized hypoxia. This affects the body's tissues and organs. Causes of asphyxia include obstruction or constriction of airways due to asthma or laryngospasm, blockage of the airway from a foreign body, or near-drowning.

Causes

Oxygen deficiency occurs when the body suffers asphyxia. The chemo-sensors of the body detect oxygen levels in the blood, and sense the need to breathe out excess carbon dioxide. Causes of asphyxiation include:

- An oxygen deficient atmosphere
- Carbon monoxide inhalation
- Chemical agents, such as hydrogen cyanide and phosgene
- Sleep apnea
- Drug overdose
- Choking
- Self-induced hypocapnia
- Seizure
- Ondine's curse (central alveolar hypoventilation syndrome)
- Acute respiratory distress syndrome

- Hanging
- Drowning

Signs and Symptoms

- Tachycardia
- Cyanosis
- Elevated blood pressure
- Seizures
- Tachypnea

Treatment and Management

- Choking: Perform Heimlich maneuver
- Drowning: Remove victim from substance/water
- Chemical/gas: Remove victim from substance, into fresh air, and administer oxygen
- Suffocation: Remove foreign object, and administer CPR
- Strangulation; Remove the object from the neck
- Asthma attack: Assist patient to the upright position, and administer rescue inhaler

Anaphylaxis

Anaphylaxis is a life-threatening allergic reaction. Once exposed to a chemical or allergen, the immune system becomes sensitized, and anaphylaxis is likely, causing the body to release histamine and other chemicals that restrict the airways.

Anaphylactic Reaction

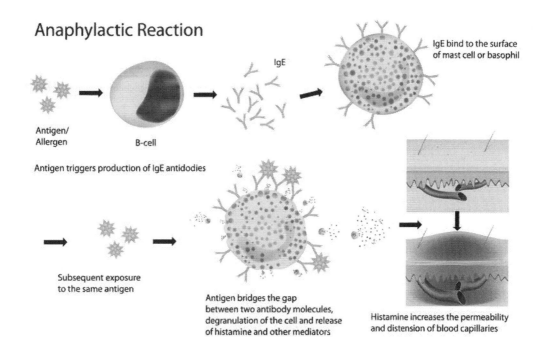

Anaphylaxis Causes

- Medications - Including antibiotics, non-steroidal anti-inflammatory drugs (NSAIDs), aspirin, and even vitamins.

- Environmental agents - Such as pollen, mold, dust, or chemicals.

- Foods - Including peanuts, shellfish, and eggs.

- Latex - Found in most medical supplies.

- Bites and stings - From wasps, bees, spiders, ants, and other insects.

Signs and Symptoms

- Anxiety

- Abnormal breathing sounds

- Chest tightness

- Cough

- Dyspnea

- Dizziness

- Dysphagia

- Hives

- Itching

- Palpitations

- Slurred speech

- Diarrhea

- Nausea and/or vomiting

- Swelling of the tongue, lips, and mouth

- Wheezing

- Loss of consciousness

Treatment and Management
- Endotracheal intubation or tracheostomy

- Oxygen

- Ventilator support

- Antihistamines

- Corticosteroids

Complications
- Respiratory arrest

- Cardiac arrest

- Shock

Multi-Organ Dysfunction Syndrome

Failure of multiple organs and systems is referred to as multi-organ dysfunction syndrome (MODS). This is caused by shock, hemorrhage, infection, burns, trauma, allergy, or severe acute pancreatitis.

Classification of MODS

- Immediate (Primary) – This type of dysfunction occurs simultaneously in two or more organs and is due to a primary disease.

- Delayed (Secondary) – This type of dysfunction occurs in a single organ, and other organs sequentially suffer failure or dysfunction.

- Accumulation – This type of dysfunction is caused by chronic disease.

Treatment and Management

- Correction of ischemia with fluid resuscitation and mechanical ventilation.

- Interruption of pathological reaction through hemofiltration.

- Prevention or treatment of infection with antibiotics and drainage.

- Stabilization of intracellular fluid by correction of electrolyte and acid-base imbalances.

- Support of organ function through dialysis, ventilator use, and cardio-protective drugs.

Sepsis and Septic Shock

Sepsis is the body's response to bacteremia or infection. Septic shock occurs when sepsis causes hypotension due to sepsis. Having certain diseases and conditions can put a patient at risk for sepsis, such as a weak immune system, heart valve abnormalities, and chemotherapy treatment.

Signs and Symptoms of Sepsis

- Tachycardia

- Hypotension

- Confusion

- Fever

- Weakness and fatigue

- Decreased urine output

Signs and Symptoms of Septic Shock

- Organ malfunction
- Hypotension that does not respond to treatment
- Cardiac arrhythmias
- Elevated BUN and creatinine
- Dyspnea
- Abnormal breath sounds

Risk Factors

- Newborn
- Being over the age of 35 years
- Pregnancy
- Chronic diseases, such as diabetes or cirrhosis
- Weak immune system
- Chemotherapy drugs
- Corticosteroid use
- Intravenous catheter
- Urinary catheter
- Breathing tube
- Injecting recreation drugs
- Artificial heart valve
- Prosthetic joint
- Persistent infection that does not respond to antibiotic therapy

Diagnosis

- Blood cultures
- CBC

- Catheter evaluation for culture

- Urine culture

- CSF evaluation

- Wound culture

- Sputum culture

- Lactic acid

- ABG

- ECG

- Chest x-ray

Treatment and Management

- Antibiotics – Sepsis and septic shock is treated immediately with broad-spectrum antibiotics, which are given before test results confirm the causative organism(s).

- Abscess drainage – Abscesses must be drained.

- Catheters and medical devices – These are removed and replaced.

- Surgery – This may be necessary to debride infected and necrotic tissue.

- IV fluids – Given to increase blood pressure and increase circulating fluid volume.

- Medications – Dopamine to increase blood flow to the heart, brain, and essential body organs.

- Supplemental oxygen – Given by nasal cannula, mask, or mechanical ventilation.

Systemic Inflammatory Response Syndrome (SIRS)

Systemic inflammatory response syndrome (SIRS) is a serious condition related to organ dysfunction and failure. It is a form of cytokine storm, which involves abnormal regulation of cytokines in the body. SIRS, like sepsis, is related to suspected or confirmed infection. This clinical condition can lead to respiratory distress syndrome, renal failure, central nervous system dysfunction, and/or gastrointestinal bleeding.

Criteria for SIRS

- Body temperature greater than 38°C(100.4°F) or less than 36°C(96.8°F)

- Tachypnea greater than 20 breaths per minute

- Arterial partial pressure of carbon dioxide less than 4.3 kPa (32 mmHg)

- Heart rate greater than 90 beats per minute

- Leukocytes less than 4,000 cells/mm³ (4×10^9 cells/L) or greater than 12,000 cells/mm³ (12×10^9 cells/L) or the presence of more than 10% immature neutrophils (left shift)

Causes of SIRS

- Infection (sepsis)

- Trauma

- Burns

- Pancreatitis

- Hemorrhage

- Ischemia

- Adrenal insufficiency

- Surgical complications

- Cardiac tamponade

- Pulmonary embolism

- Aortic aneurysm

- Anaphylaxis

- Drug overdose

Treatment and Management

- Fluid replacement to correct hypovolemia.

- IVF/NPO for pancreatitis.

- Epinephrine, corticosteroids, and antihistamines for anaphylaxis.

- Antibiotics for sepsis and infection.

Toxic Substance Ingestion

Caustic and corrosive substances can cause tissue injury, which occurs by accepting a proton (alkaline product) or donating a proton (acidic agent). The pH of a chemical substance determines if it is acidic or alkaline. To treat the patient, the CCRN must identify the specific substance ingested, the time and nature of the exposure, the duration of contact, and any treatment received.

Signs and Symptoms

- Dyspnea

- Dysphagia

- Odynophagia

- Oral pain

- Chest pain

- Abdominal pain

- Nausea and vomiting

- Tachycardia

- Tachypnea

- Hoarseness

- Stridor

- Cough

- Drooling

Indications of Severe Injury

- Altered mental status

- Viscous perforation

- Stridor

- Hypotension

- Peritoneal signs

- Shock

Diagnosis

- pH testing of the product

- pH testing of saliva

- CBC

- Electrolytes

- BUN and creatinine

- ABG

- Liver function test

- Urinalysis

- Urine output evaluation

- Type and cross blood

- ECG

- Chest x-ray

Treatment and Management

- Airway maintenance and protection

- Cardiac monitoring

- IV administration of fluids and blood as ordered

- Endoscopy if indicated

- Obtain material safety data sheet (MSDS)

- Endotracheal intubation or tracheostomy if necessary

- Gastric emptying and decontamination by gastric lavage if ordered

- NG tube suction

- Activated charcoal if ordered

Alcohol Toxicity

Toxic alcohol consumption usually refers to isopropanol, methanol, and ethylene glycol. Inebriation is associated with ataxia, slurred speech, and impaired judgment, and if levels of alcohol continue to rise, the condition can progress to CNS depression, multi-organ failure, and coma.

- Isopropanol ingestion – Can cause abdominal pain, hematemesis, and nausea.

- Methanol ingestion – Can cause ataxia, slurred speech, vision deficits, shortness of breath, headache, nausea, and anorexia.

- Ethylene glycol ingestion – This occurs in three stages:

  1. Neurologic stage (one hour after ingestion and last for up to 12 hours): Inebriation and hypocalcemia can cause muscle spasms and abnormal reflexes.

  2. Cardiopulmonary stage (12 to 24 hours after ingestion): The patient has hypertension, tachycardia, respiratory distress, and significant hypocalcemia.

  3. Renal stage (24 or more hours after ingestion): Symptoms of acute renal failure occur, and the patient can hyperventilate, suffer multiple organ dysfunction, and go into a coma.

Diagnosis

- Serum blood alcohol level

- Glucose

- CBC

- aPPT and PT

- Electrolytes

- BUN and creatinine

- Liver function tests

- Urine analysis for fluorescence

Treatment and Management

- Supportive therapy

- NG tube suctioning

- H2 blockade or proton-pump inhibitor

- Hemodialysis if indicated

- Antidotal therapy of methanol or ethylene glycol with ethanol or fomepizole

- Sodium bicarbonate infusions for metabolic acidosis

- For methanol toxicity, folinic acid at a dose of 1 mg/kg and repeat in four hours

- Monitor vital signs

- Monitor glucose levels

Drug Overdose

With a drug overdose, the side effects of that agent become more pronounced and can possibly lead to coma or death.

Signs and Symptoms

- Confusion

- Drowsiness

- Changes in vital signs

- Hypotension

- Bradycardia

- Cool, clammy skin

- Chest pain

- Shortness of breath

- Rapid, deep, slow, or shallow breathing

- Abdominal pain

- Nausea and vomiting

- Diarrhea

Diagnosis

- History and physical

- Drug screening

Treatment and Management

- Gastric lavage to remove unabsorbed substance from the stomach

- Activated charcoal is given to bind drugs and remove them.

- Physical restrains if the patient is violent or agitated.

- Endotracheal intubation

- IV, IM, or SC naloxone

- Supplemental oxygen

- Monitoring vital signs

Behavioral/Psychosocial

The CCRN must have basic knowledge of common psychosocial, behavioral, and psychiatric conditions. Early identification and treatment of risk factors, symptoms, and characteristics of these disorders can be crucial to critical care of the patient. This section covers various issues that can result in mental health problems.

Abuse, Neglect and Antisocial Behaviors

Child abuse, elder abuse, and domestic violence are problems often encountered in the healthcare setting. There are several risk factors for such abuse, including dementia, social isolation, shared living situations with an abuser, increased opportunity for contact, and exposure to perpetrators with such characteristics as drug and alcohol misuse, mental illness, and criminal history. Healthcare workers should keep these risk factors in mind when caring for children, women, and elderly patients.

Elder Abuse

According to the U.S. Census Bureau, approximately 12 percent of the population are persons 65 years old and older, and by 2050, they project that number will rise to 25 percent. Because of this increased elderly population, the number of cases of elder abuse will also increase. Elder abuse is defined as intentional actions that bring harm or serious risk of harm to a vulnerable person by a family member, trusted companion, or caregiver, and failure of the caregiver to satisfy the elderly person's basic needs and protect him or her from harm.

Categories of Elder Abuse

The National Center on Elder Abuse (NCEA) has identified seven categories of elder abuse. These are:

1. Physical abuse – This involves any act that causes injury, pain, disease, or impairment, such as pushing, striking, force-feeding, and improper use of medication or restraints.

2. Emotional and psychological abuse – This is conduct that leads to mental stress and anguish, such as threats, insults, humiliation, and isolation.

3. Neglect – This involves lack of basic needs provision, such as hygiene, eyeglasses, dentures, preventive healthcare, and safety measures.

4. Financial or material exploitation – This is misuse of the person's assets and/or money, such as stealing social security funds, possessions, and money, as well as coercion, such as assuming power of attorney and changing an existing will.

5. Sexual abuse – This involves nonconsensual intimate contact with the elderly person or exposure or similar activity when the person is not able to give consent.

6. Self-neglect – This is serious compromise to the health and safety of an elderly person by the self, enabled by the patient's right of autonomy and the physician's oath of beneficence.

7. Abandonment – This is the desertion of the elderly person by someone who has previously assumed responsibility for that person's care.

Domestic Violence

According to the U.S. Department of Health and Human Services (DHS), as many as 1 million victims of domestic violence seek treatment each year in America. Also, around 900,000 children are identified to be victims of abuse and/or neglect each year. Research suggests that approximately 30 percent of families are affected by one or both of these problems. Studies have shown that the perpetrators of domestic violence were often abused as children themselves.

Domestic violence is a pattern of assaultive and coercive behaviors that include physical, psychological, sexual, and verbal attacks, as well as economic coercion that a person uses against his or her intimate partner. This is not just one event - it is continuous pervasive or methodical use of these tactics by an abuser that wants power over the victim.

Effects of Domestic Violence on Children

Experts have identified several negative effects that domestic violence has on children. There are three categories of childhood problems directly connected to domestic violence exposure. These include:

- Cognitive and attitude problems – Poor school performance, lower cognitive functioning, limited problem-solving abilities, lack of conflict resolution skills, acceptance of violent behaviors and attitudes, and gender stereotypes.

- Behavioral, emotional, and social problems – Anger, hostility, aggression, disobedience, oppositional behavior, poor social and peer relationships, and lower self-esteem.

- Long-term consequences – Depression, post-traumatic stress disorder, and a higher tolerance for abuse and violence.

Community-Based Domestic Violence Programs

- Shelters and safe houses

- National, State, and local emergency hotlines

- Support groups

- Crisis and intervention counseling

- Legal advocacy

- Medical and mental health services

- Transportation

- Housing and relocation services

- Vocational counseling and economic support services

- Children services

Indicators of Domestic Violence

It is vital that healthcare workers and community service providers who assist in domestic violence cases assess the perpetrator's level of dangerousness. This can be done by surveying and predicting the likelihood of injury and assault. There are several risk factors to determine this form of violence. These include:

- Threats of homicide or suicide

- Use of weapons in an intimidating manner

- Possession or access to weapons

- Kidnapping

- Sexual assault

- Physical attacks

- Verbal intimidation

- Stalking behavior

- Substance abuse

- History of mental illness

- History of violence

- Police record of domestic violence

Child Abuse

Child abuse is the physical, sexual, or emotional injury, negligent treatment, or mistreatment of a child or adolescent by a person responsible for that child's health and welfare. Healthcare workers must recognize the signs and symptoms of abuse when a child enters the hospital or health facility, and should report any identified or potential abuse to appropriate authorities.

Munchausen Syndrome

Munchausen syndrome by proxy is a form of abuse or neglect where the parent or caregiver fabricates or causes a child's illness or injury, which subjects the child to unnecessary medical evaluation and treatment. This can often result in hospitalization, morbidity, or death. Mothers are more likely to display signs of this syndrome than fathers. A typical pattern consists of multiple unsubstantiated visits to physicians, hospitals, and clinics.

Inflicted Traumatic Brain Injury

Inflicted traumatic brain injury (ITBI) is commonly known as shaken baby syndrome, which is a serious form of child abuse. This occurs during the first two months of the infant's life, but can occur to infants older than this and young toddlers. Characteristic findings of ITBI include intracranial bleeding, subdural hematoma, and/or retinal hemorrhages.

Identifying Child Abuse

Several signs may alert the CCRN to potential child abuse, including:

- Burns – May have a pattern to indicate the manner, such as a cigarette or hairdryer.
- Immersion burns – May have a doughnut pattern with the central area spared from wearing a diaper or a stocking line of demarcation where the child's foot was held in water.
- Shoe prints – Where the child was kicked.
- Bite marks – Seen as an elliptical or ovoid pattern of abrasions, ecchymosis, and/or lacerations.
- Infection – Sexually abused female children may have a sexually transmitted disease (STD) or bladder infection.

Failure to Thrive

Failure to thrive (FTT) is the clinical term used to diagnose a child who is not growing within the expected range. With FTT, growth deficiency is indicated by a shifting growth pattern, such as dropping from the 80th percentile to the 10th percentile on the growth curve. The signs and symptoms of FTT include:

- Prominent rib cage
- Wasted appearance of trunk, buttocks, and thighs
- Protruding abdomen
- Sparse hair growth (worse on the back of the head)
- Pallor of the skin
- Decreased respirations, pulse, and/or blood pressure

Antisocial Behaviors, Aggression, and Violence

Antisocial behavior is any disruptive act or acts that cause hostility and aggression toward other persons. These behaviors occur along a severity continuum, which includes defiance of authority, total neglect for the rights of others, and repeated violations of social rules and the law. Antisocial people often lack empathy, have a need for admiration, are impulsive, and are excessively emotional.

Antisocial behavior is related to violence and aggression. Violence is the result of aggression, whereas aggressive behavior is based on hostility and impulsion. CCRNs should have the ability to identify patients with these behaviors to assist with care and treatment, as well as provide a safe, productive care environment.

Risk Factors for Antisocial Behaviors

- Environmental stressors
- Genetic and neurobiological factors
- History of violence
- Depression
- Schizophrenia
- Substance use/abuser

- Manic behavior

- Delirium

- Dementia

- Unstable living situations

Nursing and Medical Interventions for Antisocial Individuals

- Prevention – The best intervention is to prevent violent or aggressive behavior. The CCRN should recognize a patient who is displaying these behaviors in order to prevent antisocial behaviors.

- Referral – The patient with violence and/or aggressive tendencies should be referred to psychiatric care, social services, and community programs.

- Assessment – The patient who is at risk for antisocial behavior should be approached cautiously, and an assessment of cognition, orientation, and memory should be done to rule out delirium, dementia, and/or substance withdrawal.

- Restraints – Physical restraints are often necessary when treating patients who are violent and aggressive.

Common Disorders and Conditions

Delirium and Dementia - Overview

Delirium and dementia are two disorders that affect a patient's behavior and well-being. Approximately 15 percent of acute care hospital admission patients have delirium listed as one of the secondary diagnoses. Also, patients over the age of 80 years are at a 30 percent greater risk for dementia.

Delirium

Delirium is transient, reversible cerebral dysfunction that manifests with a wide range of neuropsychiatric signs and symptoms. Although it is more common among elderly patients, it can manifest in people of all ages.

Signs and Symptoms

- Decreased attention span
- Intermittent confusion
- Clouding of consciousness
- Disorientation
- Illusions
- Hallucinations
- Dysphasia
- Altered LOC
- Tremor
- Dysarthria
- Asterixis (with uremia and hepatic encephalopathy)
- Motor abnormalities

Diagnosis by DSM-V

- Disturbances in attention – Reduce ability to focus, sustain, and shift attention.

- Loss of conscious awareness.

- Change in cognition – Disorientation, memory deficit, perceptual disturbance, and language disturbance.

- Develops suddenly – Usually hours or a few days.

- Precipitating event or condition – Evidence from history, physical examination, and/or laboratory tests that the delirium is caused by a medical condition, medication, intoxicating substance, or more than one of these things.

Treatment and Management

The goal of treatment and management is to find the cause of delirium and correct it. This also could include supportive and pharmacologic therapy, such as:

- Fluid and nutrition – Done to correct electrolyte disturbances and dehydration.

- Vitamin supplements – Patients with a history of alcohol use may need thiamine.

- Reorientation techniques – Can include clock, calendar, and family photos.

- Environment – Quiet, well-lit, and relaxed atmosphere.

- Medications – Polypharmacy should be considered, and benzodiazepines are useful for agitated and anxious patients.

Dementia

Dementia is the loss of mental skills that affects the patient's daily life and activities of daily living. Dementia has a gradual onset and worsens over time. It is caused by damage or injury to the brain, or changes in the brain, such as tumors, strokes, or accidents. Alzheimer's disease is the most common cause of dementia.

Signs and Symptoms

- Memory loss

- Trouble recalling recent events

- Difficulty recognizing places and people

- Trouble with word usage

- Problems planning and performing certain tasks

- Judgment errors

- Difficulty controlling emotions

- Depression

- Lack of hygiene

- Visual hallucination (seen in dementia with Lewy bodies)

- Personality changes and unusual behavior (seen in frontotemporal dementia)

Diagnosis

- History and physical examination

- MMSE

- MRI of head/brain

- CT of head/brain

Treatment and Management

- Cholinesterase inhibitors – Stops the breakdown of acetylcholine (neurotransmitter), which increases the amount available in the brain to improve mental function.

- Antidepressants – SSRIs are used to treat depression.

- Stimulants – Methylphenidate can help with the symptoms of dementia and depression.

- Antipsychotics – These are used in patients with hallucinations and agitation.

- Stabilization of medical conditions – These include hypertension, heart disease, diabetes, brain tumors, headaches, hydrocephalus, hypoxia, anemia, hormone imbalances, and nutritional deficits.

- Counseling and therapy – To help with behavior problems.

Developmental Delays

For children with developmental delays, there are certain skill areas that require evaluation. The Individuals with Disabilities Education Act (IDEA) mandates that all children have the right to a proper education, regardless of disability. Areas to evaluate include: language, social-emotional, adaptive, cognitive, gross motor, and fine motor.

Children and adults with cognitive deficits are at greater risk for behavioral and psychiatric disorders than individuals in the general population. These can include issues with attention, sleep, aggression, as well as self-harming behaviors. Early detection of a developmental delay and provision of services can greatly assist the child with these problems. The medical evaluation for these children includes evaluation of cognitive impairment and genetic counseling.

Fragile X Syndrome

Fragile X syndrome is one of the leading causes of mental retardation. This condition is the result of a change in the FMR1 gene, where a small section of the gene code is repeated on a specific "fragile" area of the X chromosome. This disorder affects males more often than females, and the patient presents with hyperactive behavior, a large forehead, a prominent jaw, lack of eye contact, and mental retardation.

Down Syndrome

Down syndrome (trisomy 21) occurs when there is an error in the division of chromosomes. With proper care, the life expectancy of a person with Down syndrome is now around 60 years. These patients have broad hands, lax ligaments, a flat nasal bridge, and are short in stature. Additionally, they often keep their mouths open and have bradycardia and a short neck. When caring for a patient with this condition, CCRNs should monitor for signs and symptoms of sleep apnea, seizures, diabetes mellitus, and confusion.

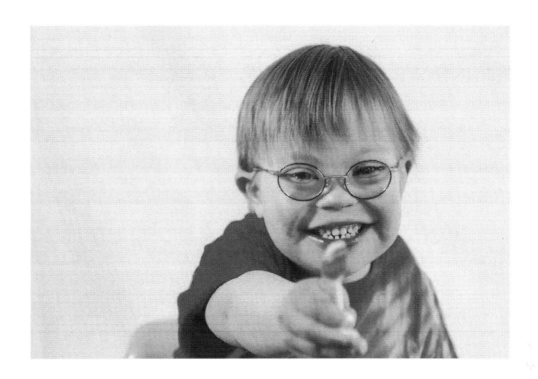

Cerebral Palsy

Cerebral palsy (CP) is a group of non-progressive conditions that lead to physical and mental disabilities. CP occurs when there is damage to the motor control centers of the brain in utero, during childbirth, or after birth. Patients with CP have motor disturbances, as well as problems with sensation, cognition, perception, behavior, and communication. Common symptoms include spasms of the face, abnormal facial gestures, decreased muscle mass, toe or scissor walking, and problems with gait and balance.

Autism Spectrum Disorder (ASD)

Autism spectrum disorder (ASD) is a blanket term used to describe a complicated developmental delay that usually presents during the first three years of life. Autism affects the ability to communicate and interact with other people. Adult patients with ASD often have a lack of language or limited communication skills, avoidance of eye contact, repetitive behaviors, and fixation on certain objects.

Testing and Evaluation of Developmental Delays

- Intelligence Quotient (IQ) Test – This gives an assessment of language development, memory, problem solving, visual-motor skills, spatial ability, and mathematical reasoning. Stable results are best seen in a child over the age of six years.

- Stanford-Binet Intelligence Scale – Used for cognitive assessment in preschool children.

- Wechsler Preschool and Primary Scale of Intelligence (WPPSI-R) – Used to assess cognitive ability in the preschool child.

- Wechsler Intelligence Scale for Children (WISC-IV) – Most commonly used test to assess cognitive ability in school-aged children.

- Vineland Adaptive Behavior Scale – Used to measure a child's level of independent functioning.

- Medical Evaluation – Lead level, thyroid function, high-resolution chromosome analysis, DNA test for fragile X syndrome, and MRI of head/brain.

Treatment and Management of Developmental Delays

Nutritional intervention is often necessary for people with specific conditions, such as galactosemia, phenylketonuria, and maple syrup urine disorder. Also, medications can be used to treat psychiatric disorders and behavior problems, such as stimulants for ADHD and ADD, antipsychotics and clonidine for aggression and irritability, and SSRIs for anxiety and/or depression.

Mood Disorders and Depression

There are four basic types of mood disorders: major depression, cyclothymia, seasonal affective disorder (SAD), and mania. Approximately 15 percent of the U.S. population has at least one depressive symptom in a given month and around 10 percent report this occurring more often. Depression is a common feature of mental illness, and people with a mood disorder are more at risk for health problems.

Depression

Depression is associated with physical health, with around 25 percent of hospitalized medical patients reporting depressive symptoms and as many as 5 percent develop major depression. Certain chronic ailments are linked to depression, such as cancer, heart disease, diabetes, hepatitis, and vitamin deficiencies. Many neurological conditions cause depression, including Alzheimer's disease, cerebrovascular accident, multiple sclerosis, and brain tumors. Additionally, moderate depressive symptoms are associated with higher rates of MI, arteriosclerosis, and hypertension.

Dysthymic Disorder

Dysthymic disorder is a form of chronic depression where the patient has a depressed mood nearly every day. The symptoms are the same as with depression, but less severe. Because dysthymic disorder is chronic, patients often respond slowly to treatment and require lifelong medications and therapy.

Bipolar Disorder

Bipolar disorder is characterized by periods of mania (highs) followed by episodes of depression (lows). A patient is diagnosed with bipolar disorder when he or she has cyclic episodes of highs and lows for more than two weeks. Many patients, however, are often misdiagnosed with this condition. A patient with bipolar disorder will complain of insomnia, fatigue, trouble focusing, relationship problems, and irritability. In the depressive state, the patient may sleep a lot, have excessive sadness, and express hopelessness and suicidal ideation. Manic patients have difficulty sleeping, and they usually have excessive energy, erratic speech and racing thoughts.

Generalized Anxiety Disorder

Generalized anxiety disorder (GAD) is a pattern of repetitive or constant worry and anxiety. Patients with GAD often complain of trouble concentrating, muscle tension, irritability, fatigue, sleep problems, and inability to control worrisome thoughts. Acute physical symptoms of anxiety include palpitations, shortness of breath, diarrhea, diaphoresis, and abdominal pain. Substance abuse, substance withdrawal, and depression are all associated with anxiety.

Depression and Physical Illness

Depression is associated with physical health, with around 25 percent of hospitalized medical patients reporting depressive symptoms and as many as 5 percent developing major depression. Certain chronic ailments are linked to depression, such as cancer, heart disease, diabetes, hepatitis, and vitamin deficiencies. Many neurological conditions cause depression, including Alzheimer's disease, cerebrovascular accident, multiple sclerosis, and brain tumors. Additionally, moderate depressive symptoms are associated with higher rates of MI, arteriosclerosis, and hypertension.

Suicidal Behavior

Suicide is the 10th leading cause of death in America, and for adolescents and young adults, it is one of the top three causes of death.

Suicide-Related Characteristics and Behaviors

- Unexpected visits to family members and friends
- Making a will and getting affairs together
- Purchasing a gun, rope, or hose
- Writing a suicide note
- Preoccupation with death
- Few friends
- Lack of association with family members
- Sense of withdrawal and/or isolation
- Lack of sense of humor (anhedonia)
- Focus on the past

Assessment of Suicide Risk

- Suicidal ideation – Determine whether the patient has thoughts of death and/or hurting self.

- Purpose of suicide – Assess if the patient is serious about not wanting to live.

- Suicide plans – Determine if the ideation involves an actual plan or specific details.

- Potential for homicide – If the patient is suicidal, assess if or not he or she also has a desire to harm others.

- Appearance – Disheveled, unkempt, or unclean clothing, as well as physical evidence of self-harm (wrist lacerations or neck rope burns).

- Affect – A flat affect.

- Thought – Command hallucinations, delusions about the benefits of suicide, and/or an obsession with taking his or her own life.

- Orientation – The presence of delirium or dementia.

Risk Factors for Suicide

- Definite plan for suicide

- Engaging in activities that indicate they are leaving life

- Strong family history of suicide

- Presence of a gun or weapon

- Psychotic symptoms

- Drug use/abuse

- Life loss (death of a loved one, loss of job, etc.)

- Major depression, anxiety, or other mood disorder

- Experiencing hallucinations

- Recent discharge from mental health facility

Suicide Intervention

- The patient cannot be left alone.

- Anything the patient could use to harm or kill himself or herself should be removed.

- The patient should be treated in a safe, secure, and supervised facility, such as inpatient mental health unit.

- The patient should be treated for underlying psychiatric conditions with appropriate medication.

Substance Abuse and Dependence

Substance abuse and dependence – including alcohol – is associated with depression and mood disorders. A dual diagnosis is when substance abuse occurs with another psychiatric condition. Stimulants, such as cocaine and methamphetamine, act on brain neurotransmitters, and this causes elation followed by serious depression. Also, alcohol and certain substances are depressants, which make a person more at risk for prolonged bouts of sadness. Patients with serious mood disorders are twice as likely to have a nicotine addiction, and stopping smoking is associated with increased depression. Chronically anxious people often medicate themselves with drugs and/or alcohol to alleviate the symptoms of anxiety and depression.

Critical care nurses often encounter patients seeking treatment for substance abuse and alcohol dependence. Also, many people with these issues end up in the intensive care unit. The nurse should strive to identify patients who need appropriate referrals for these problems, as well as know the signs of drug-seeking behavior.

Alcohol

Alcohol is a CNS depressant that acts to depress the inhibitory centers. People under the effects of alcohol will show out-of-character behaviors, impairment in rational thinking, and loss of motor coordination. The physiologic effects of chronic alcohol use include:

- GI – Peptic ulcer disease, cirrhosis, pancreatitis, and carcinoma.

- CV – Cardiomyopathy, hypertension, and atrial fibrillation.

- Neuro – Peripheral neuropathy, ataxia, Korsakoff psychosis, and dementia.

- Immunological – Suppression of neutrophil formation.

- Obstetric – Fetal alcohol syndrome, neurologic problems, and mental retardation.

- Endocrine – Impotence, gynecomastia, and testicular atrophy in men, and sexual dysfunction in women.

- Psych – Anxiety and depression.

Alcohol Withdrawal and Delirium Tremens

Alcohol withdrawal involves "the shakes," which are tremors experienced 12 to 24 hours after the patient's last drink. These tremors are related to over-excitation of the CNS and are accompanied by diaphoresis, tachycardia, insomnia, and anorexia. After 24 to 72 hours, the patient can experience generalized seizures (rum fits). Delirium tremens (DTs) begins three to five days after the last drink, and involves fever, confusion, disorientation, and visual hallucinations.

Opiates

Heroin is the most commonly abused opiate, along with prescription oxycodone, morphine, methadone, hydrocodone, fentanyl, and codeine. Intoxication from opiates causes respiratory depression and pinpoint pupils. Chronic users develop conditions such as cellulitis, skin abscesses, mycotic aneurysms, pulmonary edema, endocarditis, HIV, and various forms of hepatitis.

Opiate Withdrawal

Withdrawal from opioids can begin just a few hours after the last usage, and the onset can be delayed in patients abusing long-acting substances. The symptoms of this include diarrhea, yawning, abdominal cramps, rhinorrhea, and piloerection. These symptoms will typically peak around 48 hours and again at 72 hours, but subside after five to seven days. Heavily dependent users may have mild symptoms for up to six months, however.

Cocaine and Amphetamines

Cocaine can be inhaled, snorted, smoked, injected, or used topically. Acute intoxication leads to paranoia, tachycardia, anorexia, insomnia, agitation, elevated blood pressure, tachypnea, and diaphoresis. Chronic users often have MI, pulmonary edema, stroke, and rhabdomyolysis. Withdrawal from cocaine and amphetamines is fairly mild, with symptoms of headache, increased appetite, and depression.

Hallucinogens

Phencyclidine (PCP) causes seizures, hallucinations, muscle rigidity, seizures, and rhabdomyolysis. Anticholinergics are used for this purpose, and they lead to delirium, elevated blood pressure, tachycardia, and seizures.

Lysergic acid diethylamide (LSD), psilocybin (found in hallucinogenic mushrooms), marijuana and peyote are all in this category, but these drugs rarely cause physical symptoms or complications. A person taking LSD or mushrooms may experience significant emotional distress if they are having a "bad trip." These drugs do not have withdrawal symptoms, and do not cause physical dependency or addiction, though they can become a regular part of a patient's self-medication regimen, and thereby become more difficult for a patient to stop after chronic use.

Diagnosing Substance Abuse and Dependence

When assessing the patient, the CCRN must keep in mind that patients often underestimate their use and consumption of alcohol and/or substances. The patient should be questioned concerning their drug(s) of choice, frequency of use, amount used at one time, and method of use. Most healthcare workers use the CAGE questionnaire when assessing substance use/abuse. This includes:

- Cutting down – Has anyone ever asked you to cut down on drinking/use?

- Annoyed – Have people annoyed you by criticizing your drinking/use?

- Guilt – Do you feel guilty about your drinking/use?

- Eye opener – Have you ever had to use or drink first thing in the morning to get rid of withdrawal symptoms?

No specific laboratory tests are indicated for a patient who is seeking detoxification. However, certain studies may be conducted due to dehydration and poor nutrition, such as CBC, BUN, creatinine, electrolytes, and glucose.

Substance Abuse Treatment and Management

The patient should be placed in a treatment program under the care of a detoxification specialist. A patient with alcohol addiction may require supplementation with thiamine and folic acid. Also, benzodiazepines are often used for agitation, insomnia, and anxiety. Most often, the patient is referred to an outpatient support group, such as Narcotics Anonymous (NA) and/or Alcoholics Anonymous (AA).

Diagnosis of Behavioral and Psychosocial Conditions

There are a number of laboratory and diagnostic tests used to diagnose behavioral and psychosocial conditions.

Urine Drug Screens

Substance abuse is one of the main causes and contributors to behavioral and psychosocial problems. Urine drug screen (UDS) can help the CCRN identify risk for withdrawal, assist with determining the cause of symptoms, and assess for the potential for suicide.

Urinalysis

An elderly patient with a urinary tract infection (UTI) can present with delirium and aggressive behavior. The urinalysis is done to detect this as a potential cause of behavioral and psychosocial problems in many patients in the ICU setting.

Laboratory Tests

GGT – Elevated in chronic alcohol use/abuse.

ALT/AST – Elevated in liver dysfunction, cirrhosis, alcohol abuse, and these conditions contribute to delirium and dementia.

TSH – Elevated in hypothyroidism, which can cause depression and dementia, and low in hyperthyroidism, which can cause elation and mania.

Creatinine and BUN – Elevated in dehydration and renal insufficiency, which can cause dementia and confusion.

Electrolytes – Elevation often indicates renal dysfunction and can be a cause of dementia.

Glucose – Low levels (hypoglycemia) can cause dementia and delirium.

Cobalamin (B12) – Deficiency can lead to dementia.

Medications to Treat Behavioral and Psychosocial Conditions

Selective Serotonin Reuptake Inhibitors (SSRIs)

Selective serotonin reuptake inhibitors (SSRIs) are commonly prescribed to treat depression, dysthymic disorder, and GAD. These drugs inhibit the reuptake of serotonin, so the CNS has more available for use. Examples include Prozac, Zoloft, Celexa, and Paxil.

Selective Serotonin and norepinephrine Reuptake Inhibitors (SSNRIs)

Selective serotonin and norepinephrine reuptake inhibitors (SSNRIs) are used to treat depression and dysthymic disorder. These drugs inhibit the reuptake of both serotonin and norepinephrine. Examples include Cymbalta, Effexor, and Pristique.

Lithium

Lithium is used to treat bipolar disorder, and it alters neuronal sodium transport, which stabilizes the patient's mood. This drug only takes three to six days to work, and the patient must be monitored for diarrhea and arrhythmias.

Antipsychotics

For patients who have aggressive and violent behavior, antipsychotics are often used. These drugs work by antagonizing dopamine and serotonin receptors. Examples include olanzapine, quetiapine, and risperidone. These drugs can take up to three weeks before maximum efficiency is seen.

Benzodiazepines

Benzodiazepines are used to treat restless, anxious, aggressive, and/or violent patients. They are also used in acute alcohol withdrawal. Examples include Valium, Konopin, and Xanax. These drugs work within 30 to 60 minutes and can be administered IV for rapid effectiveness.

Professional Care and Ethical Practice

In 1975, when the American Association of Critical Care Nurses (AACN) established the Certification Corporation, it was to mandate CCRN certification. This program allows for the development, maintenance, and promotion of higher standards for critical care nursing practice, with the goal of certification as being able to provide the best patient care for critically ill individuals. This section covers the professional caring and ethical practice of nurses who function in the critical care capacity.

Advocacy/Moral Agency

Critical care nursing is the integration of knowledge, experience, skills, and individual attitudes. The nurse's competencies are essential for the care of critically ill patients and their loved ones. Clinical judgment is a part of critical care nursing, and it involves decision making, reasoning, critical thinking, and a global understanding of the patient's situation.

Advocacy and moral agency involve working on another's behalf and representing the patient's and family's concerns. The CCRN serves as a moral agent to identify and assist with ethical and clinical concerns within and outside of the clinical environment. Nurses are often the voice for those who cannot represent themselves, such as patients and family members.

Levels of Advocacy and Moral Agency

- Beginner – Advocates for self and the patient, aware of ethical conflicts, functions in own values, aware of patient rights, and accepts death as an outcome.

- Competent – Advocates for self, patient, and family members, supports ethical decisions, incorporates patient values, acknowledges the patient and family's rights, and assists with the dying process.

- Expert – Works for the patient and family, advocates for the patient and family, has resources available to use, makes decisions based on patient rights, empowers patient and family, and achieves professional relationships.

Levels of Clinical Judgment

- Beginner – Collects the basic level of data, follows written directions, and delegates decisions.

- Competent – Collects and interprets complex data, seeks help as necessary, makes routine decisions alone, recognizes certain trends and patterns, and focuses on key elements.

- Expert – Synthesizes multiple complex data, sees the global picture, collaborates with colleagues as needed, responds appropriately, and understands own limits.

Synergy Model of Patient Care

The AACN developed the Synergy Model of Patient Care in the 1990s to describe nursing practice based on eight key patient characteristics and eight nurse competencies. The main concept of this model is that the characteristics of patients and families influence and drive the competencies of nurses, and synergy results when these characteristics are matched with the nurse's competencies.

Patient Characteristics

- Resiliency

- Vulnerability

- Stability

- Complexity

- Resource availability

- Participation in care

- Participation in decision making

- Predictability

Nurse Competencies

- Clinical judgment

- Advocacy and moral agency

- Caring practices

- Collaboration

- Systems thinking

- Response to diversity

- Facilitation of learning

- Clinical inquiry

Model Assumptions

- Patients are biological, social, psychological, and spiritual entities who are at a particular developmental stage in life.

- The patient, family members, caregivers, loved ones, and community members all contribute to the nurse-patient relationship.

- The essential patient characteristics are associated with each other and cannot be viewed in isolation.

- Nurses can be described on several dimensions, and these dimensions are interrelated.

- The goal of nursing is to get the patient at his or her optimal level of wellness, and death must be an acceptable outcome when it is inevitable.

ANA Code of Ethics for Nurses

The Code of Ethics is comprised of nine provisions:

1. In all professional relationships, you must practice with compassion and respect for the inherent dignity, worth, and uniqueness of every individual, unrestricted by considerations of social or economic status, personal attributes, or the nature of their health problems.

2. Your primary commitment is to the patient, whether an individual, family, group, or community.

3. You promote, advocate for, and strive to protect the health, safety, and rights of the patient.

4. You are responsible and accountable for individual nursing practice and determine the appropriate delegation of tasks consistent with your obligation to provide optimum patient care.

5. You owe the same duties to self as to others, including the responsibility to preserve integrity and safety, to maintain competence, and to continue personal and professional growth.

6. You participate in establishing, maintaining, and improving health care environments and conditions of employment conducive to the provision of quality health care, and consistent with the values of the profession through individual and collective action.

7. You participate in the advancement of the profession through contributions to practice, education, administration, and knowledge development.

8. You collaborate with other health professionals and the public in promoting community, national and international efforts to meet health needs.

9. You recognize the value of the profession of nursing, and of maintaining the integrity of the profession and its practice, and for shaping social policy.

Caring Practices

Caring practices are nursing interventions that create a supportive, compassionate, and therapeutic environment for patients and staff with the purpose of promoting healing, comfort, and prevention of complications, disease, and suffering. These activities include engagement, vigilance, and responsiveness of caregivers, including family members, loved ones, and healthcare workers. These caring practices allow for a safe and secure environment for ill and/or injured patients[1].

Levels of Caring Practices

- Beginner – Focuses on the patient's basic needs, uses standards and protocols, and maintains a secure, safe environment.

- Competent – Responds to subtle changes, uses caring practices, optimizes the environment, and provides individualized patient care.

- Expert – Anticipates the patient' needs and health status changes, engages the family and caregivers along with the patient, and promotes comfort and safety.

Standards of Care for Acute and Critical Care Nursing

Standard of Care I: Assessment

- The nurse caring for acute and critically ill patients collects relevant patient health data. Data collection involves the patient, family, and other healthcare providers as appropriate to develop a holistic picture of the patient's needs.

- The priority of data collection activities is driven by the patient's immediate condition and/or anticipated needs.

- Pertinent data are collected using appropriate assessment techniques and instruments.

- Data are documented in a retrievable form.

- Data collection is systematic and ongoing.

---

[1] From the AACN 2014 Standards for Acute and Critical Care Nursing Practice.

Standard of Care II: Diagnosis

- The nurse caring for acute and critically ill patients analyzes the assessment data in determining diagnoses. Diagnoses are derived from the assessment data.

- Diagnoses are validated throughout the nursing interactions with a team consisting of the patient, family, and other healthcare providers, when possible and appropriate.

- Diagnoses are prioritized and documented in a manner that facilitates determining expected outcomes and developing a plan of care.

- Diagnoses are documented in a retrievable form.

Standard of Care III: Outcome Identification

- The nurse caring for acute and critically ill patients identifies individualized, expected outcomes for the patient.

- Outcomes are derived from actual or potential diagnoses.

- Outcomes are mutually formulated with the patient, family, and other health care providers, when possible and appropriate.

- Outcomes are individualized in that they are culturally appropriate and realistic in relation to the patient's age and present and potential capabilities.

- Outcomes are attainable in relation to resources available to the patient.

- Outcomes are measurable and should include a time estimate for attainment, if possible.

- Outcomes provide direction for continuity of care so that the nurse's competencies are matched with the patient's needs.

- Outcomes are documented in a retrievable form.

Standard of Care IV: Planning

- The nurse caring for acute and critically ill patients develops a plan of care that prescribes interventions to attain expected outcomes.

- The plan is individualized to reflect the patient's characteristics and needs.

- The plan is developed collaboratively with the team, consisting of the patient, family, and healthcare providers, in a way that promotes each member's contribution toward achieving expected outcomes.

- The plan reflects current acute and critical care nursing practice.

- The plan provides for continuity of care.

- Priorities for care are established.

- The plan is documented to promote continuity of care.

Standard of Care V: Implementation

- The nurse caring for acute and critically ill patients implements interventions identified in the plan of care.

- Interventions are delivered in a manner that minimizes complications and life-threatening situations.

- The patient and family participate in implementing the plan of care based upon their ability to participate in and make decisions regarding care. Interventions are documented in a retrievable manner.

Standard of Care VI: Evaluation

- The nurse caring for acute and critically ill patients evaluates the patient's progress toward attaining expected outcomes.

- Evaluation is systematic, ongoing, and criterion-based.

- The team consisting of patient, family, and healthcare providers is involved in the evaluation process as appropriate.

- Evaluation occurs within an appropriate time frame after interventions are initiated.

- Ongoing assessment data are used to revise the diagnoses, outcomes, and plan of care as needed.

- Revisions in diagnoses, outcomes, and plan of care are documented.

- The effectiveness of interventions is evaluated in relation to outcomes.

- The patient's responses to interventions are documented.

Collaboration

Collaboration involves working with patients, families, and healthcare providers to promote each person's contribution toward achieving realistic patient and family goals. This process encompasses multidisciplinary work with other healthcare professionals, community service members, patients, and families. The care environment should be one that is focused on the best interest of the patient.

Levels of Collaboration

- Beginner – Willing to learn, attend team meetings, and open to assistance.

- Competent – Willing to mentor other nurses, serves as teachers and preceptors, and involved in multidisciplinary care.

- Expert – Serves as a role model, teacher, and mentor to other nurses, facilitates team meetings, serves as a community and professional leader.

ICU Team Collaboration

Team collaboration is a professional process for patient care, decision making, and communication. The ICU team is a complex entity that relies on the needs of each moment. The core team often consists of a bedside CCRN, a respiratory therapist, and several physicians, but can include dietitians, social workers, physical therapists, and other healthcare workers. The degree of collaboration depends on each team member, and effective communication among all persons is necessary for the team to function safely, adequately, and efficiently. Nursing reports of lack of collaboration have been linked to higher rates of patient morbidity and mortality, as well as readmissions to the hospital and intensive care services.

All healthcare team providers influence the patient's care, and each team member contributes to the final care plan. The ability for two or more team members to send and receive commands and information accurately and clearly is collaborative communication, and this provides useful feedback. The team members all are responsible for problem solving, coordination of care, and patient management.

Barriers to Team Collaboration

The barriers to team collaboration include variations and differences in:

- Professions

- Language

- Training

- Status

Behaviors that Increase Risk of Patient Injury

- Lack of communication between team members

- Failure to develop and implement contingency plans

- Conflict between two or more healthcare professionals

- Poor end-of-shift report

- Tension between nurses and physicians

- Failure to anticipate potential patient health complications and problems

Facilitators for Team Collaboration

Power is the capability of one or more team members to direct, lead, offer ideas, raise concerns, and ask questions. However, power can inhibit the upward flow of necessary information. Differences in power among team members will intensify the interpersonal risk faced by members with less power. Professional status can influence beliefs about power. When a team member feels safe about asking questions and taking charge, it is considered psychological safety. This occurs without the fear of humiliation or punishment.

Improving team collaboration among ICU healthcare workers allows for patient safety and better health care. Sound decision making involves key team members making logical judgments, recognizing alternatives, and considering which ones are the best choices for the patient. To improve team collaboration, formal team training is essential, and this will decrease the number of clinical and medical errors in the ICU setting.

Other Concepts

Systems Thinking

Systems thinking is the body of knowledge and tools that allow the nurse to manage the system and environmental resources for the patient, their family, and the staff. An important aspect of systems thinking is the ability to understand how one decision will impact the whole system, so nurses must use a global perspective in clinical decision making. Additionally, critical care nurses should negotiate the needs of the patient and family members.

Levels of Systems Thinking

- Beginner – Uses standard strategies, has poor problem resolution, and understands how the nurse is a main resource.

- Competent – Provides care is based on the patient's needs, finds system solutions, reacts to patient and family needs, and negotiates decisions about care.

- Expert – The care is driven by patient and family needs, understands the entire system, navigates problems for the patient and family, and optimizes patient care outcomes.

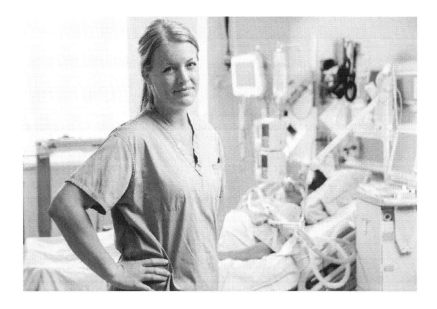

Response to Diversity

Response to diversity is an ability to recognize, appreciate, and include differences in the provision of critical patient care. Diversity can include spiritual beliefs, cultural factors, gender, ethnicity, lifestyle, race, socioeconomic status, age, and personal values. When the CCRN cares for a patient, he or she must accept the individuality of each patient and identify patterns that correlate with certain nursing interventions. Differences among people will impact their care, so the ICU environment must meet the diverse needs of each patient.

Levels of Response to Diversity

- Beginner – Assesses, understands, and uses standards, provides care based on own beliefs, and identifies barriers to patient care.

- Competent – Considers diversity's impact on patient care, accommodates for differences, assists with incorporation of system culture, and meets the patient's and family member's needs.

- Expert – Anticipates various needs of the patient and family members, incorporates differences, adapts culture to patient needs, and eliminates barriers that inhibit patient care.

Clinical Inquiry

Clinical inquiry is the continuous process of questioning and assessing practice, and giving appropriate patient care based on informed practice. The CCRN creates practice changes through experiential learning and research utilization, and clinical inquiry progresses as the nurse advances in his or her career.

Levels of Clinical Inquiry

- Beginner – Does not question current standards of practice, uses evidence-based practice as necessary, seeks assistance, and serves as a data collector.

- Competent – Adjusts standards of care to meet patient needs, applies evidence based practice, seeks alternative care measures, and serves as a research team member.

- Expert – Improves on current research, questions practice and standards, serves as a lifelong learner, and evaluates and implements evidence based practice.

Facilitation of Learning

The CCRN has the ability to facilitate learning for patients, family members, nursing staff, and healthcare workers. This is done through formal and informal teaching. Education is based on the personal strengths and weakness of those being taught.

Levels of Facilitation of Learning

- Beginner – Uses standardized learning and teaching tools and materials, provides basic patient information, and accepts the patient and family as passive learners.

- Competent – Adapts educational material and tools to the patient and family's needs, educates while providing patient care, teachers based on requirements, uses a variety of teaching methods, and allows the patient and family members to have input.

- Expert – Develops and modifies educational material, allows the patient and family members to be involved in teaching, individualizes teaching for each situation, and collaborates and negotiates teaching needs.

Practice Examination

1. **Sarah is a 58 year old Caucasian female admitted to the unit following a cardiac catheterization. She received an emergency angioplasty and now has an intra-aortic balloon pump. The inflation point is appropriate and there is a small hematoma at the insertion site. Her night was uneventful except for a headache, for which she was medicated with Tylenol #3. Her blood pressure is 135/78 and her cardiac output is 4.6. Sarah's headache is likely due to:**
   A. The pain from the procedure
   B. An intracerebral bleed
   C. The contrast dye used during the procedure
   D. The augmented blood pressure

Answer: B. An intracerebral bleed

Explanation: Sarah received anticoagulation therapy during the procedure. Following a cardiac catheterization, the CCRN monitoring the patient should notify the physician of any mental status changes or headaches, as well as changes in the size of a hematoma or oozing from the insertion site.

2. **Of the following, which conditions are associated with ST-T wave abnormalities?**
   A. Atrial hypertrophy and endocarditis
   B. Axis deviation: asthma
   C. Axis deviation: pulmonary edema
   D. COPD, ventricular hypertrophy, and pericarditis

Answer: D. COPD, ventricular hypertrophy, and pericarditis

Explanation: Atrial hypertrophy, endocarditis, asthma, and pulmonary edema do not lead to ST-T wave abnormalities. However, COPD, ventricular hypertrophy, and pericarditis do.

3. **A patient was admitted to the ICU with severe dyspnea, fatigue and malaise, all of which occurred along with an episode of syncope. The patient reports he has a mid-sternal burning sensation in the chest, and this is worse when he is supine. What does this indicate?**
   A. Myocarditis
   B. Pulmonary edema
   C. GERD
   D. Pericardial tamponade

Answer: A. Myocarditis

Explanation: Myocarditis can present with pain in the supine position and pain with inspiration. Other clinical findings are extra heart sounds (S3 and S4), a pericardial friction rub, and a recent respiratory infection.

4. **Of the following, what condition is associated with tall, peaked T waves on ECG?**
   A. Hypernatremia
   B. Hypercalcemia
   C. Hyperkalemia
   D. Hypermagnesemia

Answer: Ċ. Hyperkalemia

Explanation: With hyperkalemia, the PR interval can be prolonged, and if the potassium level is 8.0 or higher, a wide-complex tachycardia occurs. Low levels of sodium and/or calcium can potentiate these effects.

5. A 65 year-old male African American was admitted with paroxysmal nocturnal dyspnea, orthopnea, ascites, and fatigue. During his physical examination, the CCRN finds S3 and S4 gallops and basilar crackles. His ECG shows sinus tachycardia. Which type of cardiomyopathy does he have?
A. Restrictive
B. Alcohol-related
C. Dilated
D. Hypertrophic

Answer: C. Dilated

Explanation: Dilated cardiomyopathy leads to systolic dysfunction, which is associated with S3 and S4 gallops. The ECG can show sinus tachycardia, atrial fibrillation, or ventricular dysrhythmias. Patients with this type of cardiomyopathy also have ascites, peripheral edema, hepatomegaly, and pale, cool extremities.

6. Of the following, which hemodynamic effects would the CCRN expect to see in the patient with hypertrophic cardiomyopathy?
A. Normal cardiac output and an increased ejection fraction
B. Decreased cardiac output and a decreased ejection fraction
C. Decreased cardiac output and an increased ejection fraction
D. Normal cardiac output and a decreased ejection fraction

Answer: A. Normal cardiac output an increased ejection fraction

Explanation: When a patient has hypertrophic cardiomyopathy, his or her myocardium thickens at the ventricular septum rather than the ventricle or atria. A thick septum creates a hyper-dynamic state by increasing the heart's contractility, so therefore, the ejection fraction will increase.

7. Which of the following factors will compromise stroke volume?
A. Impedance, compliance, and heart rate
B. Preload, afterload, and contractility
C. Blood volume, impedance, and viscosity
D. Heart rate, blood pressure, and cardiac output

Answer: B. Preload, afterload, and contractility

Explanation: Blood volume, impedance, and viscosity (choice C) are components of afterload. Impedance, compliance, heart rate, and blood pressure are mixed components of cardiac output. The factors that compromise stroke volume are impedance, compliance, and heart rate.

8. The coronary artery that encircles the heart is called the:
A. Posterior descending artery
B. Right coronary artery
C. Circumflex artery
D. Circumflexion artery

Answer: C. Circumflex artery

Explanation: The circumflex artery supplies the posterior descending artery in left dominant coronary circulation and encircles the heart. The right coronary artery supplies the posterior descending artery in right dominant coronary circulation. Co-dominant circulation is when the posterior descending artery is supplied by both the circumflex and the right coronary arteries.

9. What percentage of water is plasma?
A. 50%
B. 51%
C. 90%
D. 91%

Answer: D. 91%

Explanation: Plasma contains 91% water.

10. The fibrous sac around the heart is called the:
A. Epicardium
B. Myocardium
C. Pericardium
D. Endocardium

Answer: C. Pericardium

Explanation: The endocardium is the smooth lining inside the heart. The myocardium is the thick muscular heart wall. The epicardium is the outer layer of the heart and inner layer of pericardium. The pericardium is the fibrous sac around the heart.

11. What is the name of the pacemaker that is considered the "back-up," and how many beats per minute does it generate?
A. Sinoatrial (SA) node, 60 to 100 beats per minute
B. Sinoatrial (SA) node, 20 to 40 beats per minute
C. Atrioventricular (AV) junction, 60 to 100 beats per minute
D. Atrioventricular (AV) junction, 40 to 60 beats per minute

Answer: D. Atrioventricular (AV) junction, 40 to 60 beats per minute

Explanation: The heart has a conduction (electrical) system, which generates electrical impulses and stimulates heart muscle contraction. The primary area is the sinoatrial (SA) node, which generates anywhere from 60 to 100 impulses per minute in the adult. The backup pacemaker is the atrioventricular (AV) junction, which generates electrical impulses at around 40 to 60 per minute. The bundle of His is a pacemaker that can generate around 20 to 40 impulses per minute.

12. The pre-contraction pressure that is based on the amount of blood that flows back to the heart is called:
A. Preload
B. Afterload
C. Contractility
D. Blood volume

Answer: A. Preload

Explanation: Myocardial contractility is the ability of the heart to contract, which requires adequate blood volume and muscle strength. Preload is the pre-contraction pressure based on the amount of blood that flows back to the heart. An increased preload leads to increased ventricular stretching of the ventricles and increased contractility. Afterload is the resistance which the heart must overcome during contraction of the ventricles. If there is an increase in afterload, there is decreased cardiac output.

13. Of the following, which is the correct path of blood flow?
A. The right atrium pumps blood into the left atrium, which then pumps oxygen-poor blood the pulmonary veins into the lungs. When oxygenated, the pulmonary arteries return the blood to the left ventricle.
B. The right ventricle pumps blood into the left ventricle, which then pumps oxygen-poor blood the pulmonary arteries into the lungs. When oxygenated, the pulmonary veins return the blood to the right ventricle.
C. The right atrium pumps blood into the right ventricle, which then pumps oxygen-poor blood the pulmonary arteries into the lungs. When oxygenated, the pulmonary veins return the blood to the left atrium.
D. The left atrium pumps blood into the left ventricle, which then pumps oxygen-poor blood the pulmonary arteries into the lungs. When oxygenated, the pulmonary veins return the blood to the right ventricle.

Answer: C. The right atrium pumps blood into the right ventricle.

Explanation: The vena cava returns blood to the right atrium, which pumps into the right ventricle. The right ventricle pumps oxygen-poor blood to the pulmonary arteries and then to the lungs. Carbon dioxide and oxygen exchange between the alveoli and capillaries, and the lungs send oxygen-rich blood to the heart via the pulmonary veins. Blood enters the left atrium which pumps blood to the left ventricle, and from there, it enters the aorta for circulation.

14. **Of the following, which is true concerning systemic vascular resistance (SVR)?**
A. Constriction increases vessel size and increases SVR.
B. Dilation increases vessel size and lowers SVR.
C. Constriction reduces vessel size and lowers blood pressure.
D. Dilation increases vessel size and increases blood pressure.

Answer: B. Dilation increases vessel size and lowers SVR.

Explanation: Systemic vascular resistance (SVR) is a resistance to blood flow in the body, but this excludes the pulmonary system. SVR is related to the blood vessel size. Constriction reduces vessel size, which increases SVR and blood pressure. Dilation increases vessel size, which lowers SVR and blood pressure.

15. **Which drug is not considered a diuretic?**
A. Furosemide
B. Mannitol
C. Ethacrynic acid
D. Atenolol

Answer: D. Atenolol

Explanation: Diuretics include furosemide and ethacrynic acid (loop diuretics), mannitol (osmotic diuretics), HCTZ (thiazides), and amiloride hydrochloride and spironolactone (potassium-sparing diuretics).

16. **Which preload reduction agent is used to reduce acute hypertension and for afterload reduction in patients with heart failure?**
A. Nitroglycerin
B. Nitroprusside
C. Mannitol
D. Esmolol

Answer: B. Nitroprusside

Explanation: Coronary vasodilators are preload reduction agents that are used to treat myocardial pain and relax smooth muscle. Nitroprusside is used to reduce acute hypertension and for afterload reduction in patients with heart failure. Nitroglycerin reduces filling pressure and dilates the coronary arteries. Mannitol is an osmotic diuretic, and esmolol is a beta blocker.

17. **Which afterload reduction agents reduce afterload and cause vasodilation, which in turn, decreases the left ventricle's workload, as also block the conversion of angiotensin I to angiotensin II?**
A. Angiotensin-converting enzyme inhibitors (ACEIs)
B. Angiotensin II receptor blockers (ARBs)
C. Hydralazine
D. Vasopressors

Answer: A. Angiotensin-converting enzyme inhibitors (ACEIs)

Explanation: Angiotensin-converting enzyme inhibitors (ACEIs) reduce afterload and cause vasodilation, which in turn, decreases the left ventricle's workload. They also block the conversion of angiotensin I to angiotensin II. Hypotension is a complication of ACEIs, and examples include enalapril and captopril. Angiotensin II receptor blockers (ARBs) work much like ACEIs. They block the effects of angiotensin II (chemical that contracts vessels), and dilate vessels to decrease blood pressure. Irbesartan, losartan, and valsartan are ARBs that work well for patient s with heart failure, hypertension, and those who cannot take ACEIs. Hydralazine is a potent arterial smooth muscle dilator that is given IV. Vasopressors are sympathomimetic drugs that control peripheral vasoconstriction and increase afterload and systemic vascular resistance. Three common vasopressors are norepinephrine, neosynephrine, and vasopressin.

18. What would be the correct loading dose for Milirinone?
A. 50 mcg/kg over 10 minutes
B. 25 mcg/kg over 10 minutes
C. 10 mcg/kg over 20 minutes
D. 5.0 mcg/kg over 20 minutes

Answer: A. 50 mcg/kg over 10 minutes

Explanation: Inotropic drugs improve cardiac contractility and improve cardiac output. Milirinone relaxes the smooth muscle of vessels and increases myocardial contractility. The loading dose is 50 mcg/kg over 10 minutes followed by IV infusion of 0.375 to 0.75 mcg/kg/minute. Others are digoxin and dobutamine.

19. What class of anti-arrhythmic agents is metoprolol and propranolol?
A. Class 1A
B. Class 1B
C. Class II
D. Class III

Answer: C. Class II

Explanation: Anti-arrhythmic agents are classified as Class I through IV. The class of drug depends on the drug's action. Class 1A – Quinidine and procainamide (sodium channel blockers). Class IB – Lidocaine (sodium channel blocker). Class II – Metoprolol and propranolol (beta blockers). Class III – Amiodarone (slow depolarization). Class IV – Diltiazem and verapamil (calcium channel blockers). Unclassified – Adenosine and magnesium.

20. **Rachel suffered a cardiac arrest while shopping. CPR did not begin until five minutes later, when the paramedics arrived. Rachel was pulseless, in ventricular tachycardia during transport, and the paramedics performed continuous CPR. When admitted to the ICU, the physician ordered hypothermic measures and vecuronium. Why is this medication used?**
A. To relieve pain
B. To sedate the patient
C. To prevent shivering
D. To control ventricular dysrhythmias

Answer: C. To prevent shivering

Explanation: Vecuronium is a paralytic agent that will prevent shivers, so the patient's body temperature will not rise.

21. **If the patient in ICU develops cardiac tamponade, what triad of symptoms will you see, and what will show on the chest x-ray?**
A. Hypertension, tachycardia, and right ventricular failure; increased JVD
B. Muffled heart sounds, hypotension, and dilated neck veins; dilated supra vena cava
C. Tachycardia, hypotension, and left ventricular failure; delineation of the pericardium
D. Increased JVD, elevated pulse pressure, and tachycardia; narrowed mediastinum

Answer: B. Muffled heart sounds, hypotension, and dilated neck veins; dilated supra vena cava

Explanation: Beck's triad includes muffled heart sounds, hypotension, and dilated neck veins. Tachycardia is an early sign, and a narrowed pulse pressure occurs when the fluid does not leave the heart. The chest x-ray will show a dilated superior vena cava because blood does not empty into the right atrium as it should. JVD is not visible on an x-ray, the mediastinum is widened, not narrowed, and there is no delineation of the pericardium with tamponade.

22. The main trigger for coronary thrombosis is:
A. Inflammatory cells
B. Hypotension
C. Coronary obstruction
D. Plaque rupture

Answer: D. Plaque rupture

Explanation: Acute coronary syndrome (ACS) occurs when there is high-grade coronary obstruction, which often results from emotional stress, dehydration, infection, hypotension, thyrotoxicosis, or surgery. The main trigger for coronary thrombosis is plaque rupture, which occurs due to dissolution of the fibrous cap and release of the activated inflammatory cells. After this event, platelet activation, platelet aggregation, coagulation pathway activation, and vasoconstriction occur

23. When diagnosing angina, what should you look for?
A. ST depressions
B. Transient ST-segment elevations
C. T wave changes
D. All of the above

Answer: D. All of the above

The most important diagnostic test for angina in the emergency setting is electrocardiogram (ECG). In the unit setting, telemetry monitoring often is involved with diagnosis. ECG changes seen during an episode of angina include: ST depressions (may be down sloping, horizontal, or junctional), transient ST-segment elevations, and T wave changes, such as normalizations, inversions, or hyper-acute changes.

24. Of the following patients, which one is NOT a candidate for percutaneous coronary intervention (PCI)?

A. A 38 year-old white male with NSTEMI, recurrent angina, and ST-segment depression.

B. A 56 year-old Asian female with NSTEMI and no high-risk factors.

C. A 67 year-old African-American male with STEMI and a new left bundle branch block.

D. A 44 year-old white female with sustained ventricular tachycardia, hemodynamic instability and ST-elevation MI.

Answer: B. A 56 year-old Asian female with NSTEMI and no high-risk factors.

Explanation: The preferred treatment for ST-elevation MI is percutaneous coronary intervention (PCI). Patients with MI or STEMI with a new left bundle branch block need to have PCI within 90 minutes of the event. PCI is also necessary for those patients with NSTEMI and high-risk factors, such as recurrent angina, elevated cardiac enzymes, ST-segment depression, sustained ventricular tachycardia, hemodynamic instability, and history of PCI or bypass surgery.

25. Which of the following is NOT a risk factor for acute myocardial infarction (AMI)?

A. Diabetes

B. Dyslipidemia

C. Obesity

D. Hypertension

Answer: C. Obesity

Explanation: Risk factors for AMI include age, diabetes, smoking, dyslipidemia, hypertension, and family history.

26. A factor that determines the severity of an MI is:
A. The length of time of the occlusion
B. The level of the occlusion
C. The presence of absence of collateral circulation
D. All of the above

Answer: D. All of the above

Explanation: The three factors that determine the severity of an MI are: the length of time of the occlusion (the longer the period of occlusion, the greater the chances of myocardial cell and tissue death); the level of the occlusion (the more proximal the occlusion, the more extensive the tissue necrosis); and the presence or absence of collateral circulation.

27. What drug class or agent is given within 12 hours of AMI symptoms to decrease the incidence of ventricular arrhythmias, reinfarction, recurrent ischemia, and infarct size?
A. Nitrates
B. Beta blockers
C. Morphine
D. Antiplatelet agents

Answer: B. Beta blockers

Explanation: Nitrates are given for vasodilation of coronary arteries, but are contraindicated when a patient has severe pump dysfunction or residual ischemia. Morphine is the opiate drug of choice for pain control, and it also assists with vasodilation. An antiplatelet agent, such as aspirin, is given to interfere with the function of cyclooxygenase and prevent the formation of a thromboxane A2, and prevents platelet aggregation and adhesion. Several studies recommend the use of clopidogrel along with aspirin. A beta blocker, such as atenolol, is given within 12 hours of AMI symptoms to decrease the incidence of ventricular arrhythmias, reinfarction, recurrent ischemia, and infarct size.

28. The typical maintenance dose of unfractionated heparin following an AMI is:
A. 60 U/kg/hr IV
B. 16 U/kg/hr IV
C. 12 U/kg/hr IV
D.   6 U/kg/hr IV

Answer: C. 12 U/kg/hr IV

Explanation: The loading dose of unfractionated heparin is 60 U/kg IV bolus, and the maintenance dose is 12 U/kg/hr IV.

29. Of the following patients, which one is more likely to develop or have carotid artery stenosis?
A. A 72 year-old white male who exercises regularly, has normal blood pressure and lipids, and does not smoke.
B. A 72 year-old white female who exercises regularly, has normal blood pressure and lipids, and does not smoke.
C. A 58 year-old Asian male who smokes and has normal cholesterol.
D. A 58 year-old African American female who has hypertension but does not smoke.

Answer: C. A 58 year-old Asian male who smokes and has normal cholesterol.

Explanation: Older patients are more likely to have carotid stenosis, with men more at risk than women. A person who has an elevated lipid profile, hypertension, and smokes is 8x more likely to develop carotid artery stenosis.

30. The carotid angioplasty and stenting procedure is usually done when the patient has what percent or greater of stenosis?

A. 20%

B. 40%

C. 50%

D. 70%

Answer: D. 70%

Explanation: Carotid angioplasty/stenting is done by a minimally invasive procedure where the plaque is compressed to widen the artery lumen. This is done during an angiogram with a flexible catheter that is inserted in the femoral artery. This procedure is reserved for patients with moderate to high-grade stenosis greater than 70 percent, or for patients who have multiple risk factors.

31. Acute pulmonary edema occurs from increased capillary hydrostatic pressure that is due to elevated pulmonary venous pressure. This causes accumulation of _____ in the lung interstitium?

A. Lymphatic cell fluid

B. Low-protein fluid

C. High-protein fluid

D. Extracellular fluid

Answer: B. Low-protein fluid

Explanation: Also called cardiogenic pulmonary edema (CPE), acute pulmonary edema occurs from increased capillary hydrostatic pressure that is due to elevated pulmonary venous pressure. This causes accumulation of low-protein fluid in the lung interstitium and alveoli.

32. In the patient with pulmonary edema, what causes left ventricular (LV) diastolic dysfunction?
A. Severe anemia, excessive sodium intake, and sepsis
B. Myocardial toxins, aortic stenosis, and mitral valve regurgitation
C. Ischemia, infarction, pericarditis, and tamponade
D. Aortic regurgitation, acute MI, and thyrotoxicosis

Answer: C. Ischemia, infarction, pericarditis, and tamponade

Explanation: With LV systolic dysfunction, chronic LV failure is exacerbated by severe anemia, acute MI, excessive sodium intake, noncompliance with medications, thyrotoxicosis, sepsis, myocarditis, myocardial toxins, aortic stenosis, mitral regurgitation, and aortic regurgitation. With LV diastolic dysfunction, LV diastolic dysfunction is caused by ischemia, infarction, pericarditis, and tamponade.

33. IABP is done to stabilize the patient in pulmonary edema. What does this stand for?
A. Intra-aortic balloon pumping
B. Intra-arterial balloon pumping
C. Invasive aortic basic pumping
D. Invasive arterial body pumping

Answer: A. Intra-aortic balloon pumping

Explanation: Intra-aortic balloon pumping (IABP) is done for hemodynamic stabilization in the patient with CPE.

34. Blunt cardiac injury with ischemic changes and heart block without cardiac failure, or penetrating cardiac wound without tamponade, are criteria for which grade of cardiac injury, according to the American Association for the Surgery of Trauma (AAST)?
A. Grade I
B. Grade II
C. Grade III
D. Grade IV

Answer: B. Grade II

Explanation: The grades of the AAST Injury Scale include:

- Grade I: Blunt cardiac injury with minor ECG changes, such as nonspecific ST and T wave changes, persistent sinus tachycardia, premature ventricular contractions, and premature atrial contractions.
- Grade II: Blunt cardiac injury with ischemic changes or heart block without cardiac failure; or penetrating cardiac wound without tamponade.
- Grade III: Blunt cardiac injury with multifocal ventricular contractions; blunt pericardial laceration; blunt or penetrating injury with septal rupture, papillary muscle dysfunction, pulmonary or tricuspid incompetence, or distal coronary artery occlusion without cardiac failure; or penetrating myocardial wound with tamponade.
- Grade IV: Blunt or penetrating cardiac injury with septal rupture, papillary muscle dysfunction, pulmonary or tricuspid incompetence, or distal coronary artery occlusion that produces cardiac failure; blunt or penetrating cardiac injury with aortic or mitral valve incompetence; and blunt or penetrating cardiac injury of the right ventricle, right atrium, or left atrium.
- Grade V: Blunt or penetrating cardiac injury with proximal coronary artery occlusion; blunt or penetrating left ventricular perforation; or stellate injuries with less than 50 percent tissue loss of the right ventricle, right atrium, or left atrium.
- Grade VI: Blunt avulsion of the heart; or penetrating would that produces more than 50 percent tissue loss of one or more chambers.

35. The CCRN is treating an ICU patient who has recently suffered an acute MI. He is having runs of premature ventricular contractions and his vital signs show a low blood pressure and elevated heart rate. The nurse notices his extremities have recently became mottled and cool, and his urine output is only 60 cc over the last three hours. What should the CCRN suspect?

A. Cardiac tamponade
B. Cardiomyopathy
C. Cardiogenic shock
D. Diabetic ketoacidosis

Answer: C. Cardiogenic shock

Explanation: Cardiogenic shock is decreased cardiac output that leads to tissue hypoxia, and it is the leading cause of death for patients who suffer AMI, with mortality rates of around 85 percent when the patient does not receive adequate technical care. The signs and symptoms of cardiogenic shock include hypotension, hypovolemia, oliguria, cyanosis, altered mentation, mottled, cool extremities, faint, rapid peripheral pulses, arrhythmias, low pulse pressure, tachycardia, and decreased urine output.

36. The property of cardiac cells that allows them to send electrical impulses and occurs when cells alter their membranes to attract NA+ is called:

A. Contractility
B. Excitability
C. Automaticity
D. Conductivity

Answer: C. Automaticity

Explanation: Automaticity is the physiological property of the cardiac cells that allow them to send the electrical impulse. This action occurs when cells alter their membranes and attract sodium (NA+) into them. Contractility is the physiological property of cardiac cells that allows the cell to pump blood in response to the stimulus. Excitability is the physiological property of the cardiac cells that allows the cell to respond to the impulse. Conductivity is the physiological property of the cardiac cells that allows each cell to put off the impulse.

37. Which ECG finding represents ventricular repolarization, and measures < 5 mm high?
A. P wave
B. Q wave
C. T wave
D. U wave

Answer: C. T wave

Explanation: The P wave represents atrial depolarization and is < 0.10 seconds wide and < 3 mm high. The Q wave is < 0.04 seconds wide and < 3 mm deep. The R wave is < 7.5 mm high. The T wave represents ventricular repolarization, and measures < 5 mm high. The U wave represents ventricular after-potential, and is any deflection after the T wave.

38. With this form of heart block, the electrical impulse moves through the AV node slowly, and the heart beat is at a slow rate, causing dizziness for some patients. Drugs used to treat this block include beta blockers, calcium channel blockers, and digoxin. What is it?
A. Bundle branch block (BBB)
B. First degree heart block
C. Second degree heart block
D. Third degree heart block

Answer: B. First degree heart block

Explanation: With BBB, when there is a block in the right or left branches, impulses must travel to the affected side by way of a detour, which indicates that one of the ventricles is contracting a fraction of a second slower than the other one. With first degree heart block, the electrical impulse moves through the AV node slowly, and the heart beat is at a slow rate. Second degree heart block occurs when electrical impulses from the atria do not reach the ventricles, and there is dropped beats on the ECG. Also called complete heart block, third degree heart block occurs when the electrical impulse does not pass from the hearts atria to the ventricles at all, and secondary pacemaker cells must take over, and this causes the ventricles to contract at a slower rate.

39. **Roger is a 27 year-old engineer who has been on hemodialysis for 4 years. He missed the last two scheduled treatments, and now is lethargic, confused, extremely fatigued, and is very edematous. According to his ABGs, his PaCO2 is 34 mmHg, his PaO2 is 68 mmHg, his pH is 7.35, and his HCO3 is 18 mEq/L. What do these results indicate?**
A. Respiratory acidosis
B. Respiratory alkalosis
C. Metabolic acidosis
D. Metabolic alkalosis

Answer: C. Metabolic acidosis

Explanation: These ABG results show an uncompensated metabolic acidosis, as the pH and the PaO2 values are both low.

40. **Shawn is a 42 year-old construction worker who recently fell from a scaffold and suffered a flail chest. He was first ventilated using a high-frequency jet ventilator, and is now on the SIMAV mode. Orders to day are to start the weaning process. What indicators would show that Shaw could be failing the weaning process?**
A. The SpO2 is 97%.
B. The heart rate has increased from 78 to 110.
C. The minute ventilation is 8 L/min.
D. His respiratory rate increased by 9 breaths per minute.

Answer: B. The heart rate has increased from 78 to 110.

Explanation: An increased heart rate is an indicator of failure to wean from the ventilator. If the PaO2 level drops or the minute ventilation is increased to more than 10 L/min, the patient is also considered to have failed weaning.

41. Ralph was admitted to the unit following a fall from a deck on the back of his house. He is having stabbing substernal pain each time he deep breathes or changes position. He was diagnosed with pneumomediastinum, so which common significant finding would the CCRN expect to see?
A. Cullen's sign
B. Hande's sign
C. Grey-Turner sign
D. Hamman's sign

Answer: D. Hamman's sign

Explanation: A crunching or slight clicking sound with each heart sound over the apex is considered Hamman's sign. This is associated with pneumomediastinum.

42. Which type of pneumonia occurs in a patient who has risk factors of age older than 65 years, chronic conditions such as diabetes, renal failure, and diabetes, a weak immune system, and antibiotic resistance, and for which typical causative microorganisms are *Streptococcus pneumonia, Moraxella catarrhalis*, and *Haemophilius influenzae?*
A. Community-acquired pneumonia (CAP)
B. Hospital-acquired pneumonia (HAP)
C. Nosocomial pneumonia
D. Atypical pneumonia

Answer: A. Community-acquired pneumonia (CAP)

Explanation: Hospital-acquired pneumonia (HAP), previously known as nosocomial pneumonia, is a pneumonia that occurs at least 72 hours after the patient is admitted to the hospital. The pathogens inside the hospital are more antibiotic resistant, so patients are usually treated with two or three different types of antibiotics. Community-acquired pneumonia (CAP) is pneumonia that occurs in a patient who has not recently been in the hospital. The typical microorganisms are *Streptococcus pneumonia, Moraxella catarrhalis*, and *Haemophilius influenzae*. The atypical pathogens include the *Mycoplasma* species and *Chlamydophila pneumoniae*.

43. Bronchiolitis typically affects:
A. Adults with COPD
B. Adults with compromised immune systems
C. Children under the age of five years old
D. Children under the age of two years old

Answer: D. Children under the age of two years old

Explanation: Bronchiolitis is edema of the bronchioles associated with mucus accumulation, usually secondary to viral pathogen. Bronchiolitis typically affects young children under the age of two, and is commonly caused by the respiratory syncytial virus (RSV). Other viruses that cause bronchiolitis are the adenovirus, parainfluenza and influenza, and the infection is spread by droplet transmission.

44. A 16 year-old female with cystic fibrosis was admitted to the ICU with acute pneumonia. She is currently experiencing sharp chest pain that is worse with inhalation or coughing, dyspnea, cyanosis, chest tightness, and fatigue. Her vital signs show: temperature 99.0, heart rate is 120, blood pressure 144/100, and respirations of 24. What is she likely experiencing?
A. An acute exacerbation of the cystic fibrosis
B. Typical pneumonia symptoms
C. A pneumothorax
D. A pneumopericardium

Answer: C. A pneumothorax

Explanation: With a pneumothorax, the pressure affects lung expansion when the patient takes a deep breath. With a spontaneous pneumothorax, a bleb breaks open and sends air into the space around the lung. Risk factors include cystic fibrosis, COPD, asthma, whooping cough, and tuberculosis. All symptoms the patient is experiencing are indicative of pneumothorax, as is tachycardia and nasal flaring.

45. For the patient who has aspirated a foreign body, what would be the FIRST thing the CCRN should do?
A. Check to see if the foreign body is in the airway.
B. Notify the physician.
C. Call a code.
D. Send the patient for a chest x-ray

Answer: A. Check to see if the foreign body is in the airway.

Explanation: Aspiration of a foreign body is a life-threatening emergency. The object can become lodged in the trachea or larynx, and can cause complete obstruction of the airway, leading to death. When treating an aspiration of a foreign object, if the choking and coughing resolves, and the patient does not have any symptoms or signs of infection, report the incident to the attending physician. A chest x-ray may be warranted, and a bronchoscopy is done to confirm the diagnosis and remove the foreign body from the airway. Antibiotics are usually given as a precautionary measure.

46. Which medications are used as control agents for the patient with asthma?
A. Inhaled corticosteroids and leukotriene modifiers
B. Inhaled albuterol and IV corticosteroids
C. Inhaled levalbuterol and IV theophylline
D. All of the above

Answer: A. Inhaled corticosteroids and leukotriene modifiers

Explanation: For asthma, control agents include inhaled corticosteroids, long-acting bronchodilators, inhaled cromolyn or nedocromil, leukotriene modifiers, and theophylline. Quick acting agents are albuterol and Levalbuterol. To treat exacerbations, inhaled nebulizer and IV corticosteroids are used.

47. **Which type of pulmonary hypertension (PH) is caused by lung disease, sleep apnea, and pulmonary abnormalities that result in low oxygen levels?**
A. Arterial PH
B. Venous PH
C. Hypoxic PH
D. Thromboembolic PH

Answer: C. Hypoxic PH

Explanation: Pulmonary hypertension (PH) is increased blood pressure in the lung vessels, and it is caused by restriction of the pulmonary arteries, blood clots in the pulmonary vessels, or fibrosis of these vessels. Arterial PH is caused by restriction of the blood arterial vessels leading to the lungs and inside the lungs. Venous PH is caused when the left side of the heart does not pump adequately and pulmonary edema and effusions develop. Hypoxic PH is caused by lung disease, sleep apnea, and pulmonary abnormalities that result in low oxygen levels. Thromboembolic PH is caused by blood clots in the pulmonary vessels. Miscellaneous PH is caused by various diseases, such as sarcoidosis and lung tumors.

48. **This procedure involves the use of a special scope (a lighted instrument) to biopsy lymph nodes for patients with suspected lung cancer, or to investigate masses:**
A. Bronchoscopy
B. Mediastinoscopy
C. Pleural biopsy
D. Thoracoscopy

Answer: B. Mediastinoscopy

Explanation: Diagnostic bronchoscopy involves the use of a flexible instrument to directly visualize the lung or airway lesion for biopsy. Mediastinoscopy involves the use of a mediastinoscope (a lighted instrument) to biopsy the lymph nodes for patients with suspected lung cancer or to investigate masses. Pleural aspiration and biopsy is done to remove fluid from a pleural effusion with a needle and syringe. Video-assisted thoracoscopy is done using a camera and scope, so the surgeon can inspect the pleural space, mediastinum, and lung, and take material from lesions.

49. **What hormone moves glucose from the blood into the liver, muscle, and fat cells so it can be used for fuel?**
A. Serotonin
B. Glucagon
C. Insulin
D. Antidiuretic hormone (ADH)

Answer: C. Insulin

Explanation: Glucose enters the bloodstream from the food and this stimulates the pancreas to release insulin. The hormone insulin should move the glucose from the blood into the liver, muscle, and fat cells so it can be utilized for fuel. However, people with diabetes cannot move the glucose appropriately because their pancreas does not produce any or enough insulin and/or their cells do not respond normally to the insulin.

50. **Which of the following is an appropriate treatment for type I diabetes mellitus?**
A. NPH rapid-acting insulin before breakfast and dinner
B. Long-acting insulin before breakfast in the am and a rapid-acting insulin before meals and snacks
C. Regular insulin after each meal and after each snack
D. Rapid-acting insulin infused intermittently via an insulin pump

Answer: B. Long-acting insulin before breakfast and a rapid-acting insulin prior to all meals and snacks thereafter

Explanation: Appropriate type 1 diabetes treatment involves:

- Split or mixed – NPH rapid-acting (lispro, glulisine, or aspart) or regular insulin before breakfast and dinner.
- Split or mixed variant – NPH rapid-acting or regular insulin before breakfast, rapid-acting or regular insulin before dinner, and NPH before bedtime.
- Multiple daily injections – Long-acting insulin (detemir or glargine) once daily in the am or evening and a rapid-acting insulin before meals and snacks.
- Continuous subcutaneous insulin infusion (CSI) – Rapid-acting insulin infused continuously via insulin pump.

51. Of the following, which is considered an exogenous cause of hypoglycemia?
A. Pancreatic tumor
B. Dumping syndrome
C. Prolonged muscle use from exercise
D. Alcohol use

Answer: D. Alcohol use

Explanation: Endogenous causes include pancreatic tumors, insulinomas, and inborn metabolic errors. Exogenous causes include insulin secretagogues, insulin excess, alcohol use, oral antidiabetic agents, and certain drugs (pentamidine and salicylates). Functional causes include dumping syndrome, prolonged muscle use from seizure or exercise, and spontaneous reactive hypoglycemia.

52. Which type of diabetes insipidus (DI) results from abnormal amounts of water, which suppresses ADH release and causes polyuria, and is caused by psychoses or an impaired thirst mechanism?
A. Nephrogenic DI
B. Neurogenic DI
C. Dipsogenic DI
D. Pathogenic DI

Answer: C. Dipsogenic DI

Explanation: Nephrogenic DI is caused by an inadequate response of the kidneys to ADH, which is peripheral and related to drug toxicity or kidney conditions. This is caused by sarcoidosis, amyloidosis, polycystic kidney disease, multiple myeloma, nephrotoxic drugs, or sickle cell disease. Neurogenic DI occurs from damage to the posterior pituitary gland from trauma or growths. This leads to insufficient amounts of ADH and an inadequate renal response. Dipsogenic DI is considered primary polydipsia, and this type of DI results from abnormal amounts of water, which suppresses ADH release and causes polyuria. This is caused by psychoses or an impaired thirst mechanism. There is no pathogenic DI.

53. **An important aspect of treatment for diabetic ketoacidosis (DKA) is fluid resuscitation. Which would be the best option?**
A. 0.45% NS
B. D5 ½ NS
C. 0.9% NS
D. 1.5% NS

Answer: C. 0.9% NS

Explanation: Diabetic ketoacidosis (DKA) is a life-threatening condition that occurs in diabetic patients. This condition is characterized by ketoacidosis, hyperglycemia, and ketonuria. Fluid resuscitation involves administering 0.9% NS 1 liter the first hour, then 300-500 mL per hour for several hours.

54. **Of the following symptoms and signs, which is NOT associated with syndrome of inappropriate secretion of antidiuretic hormone (SIADH)?**
A. Concentrated urine
B. Confusion
C. Hyponatremia
D. Hyporeflexia

Answer: A. Concentrated urine

Explanation: SIADH is hyponatremia and hypo-osmolality that occurs from continued secretion or action of antidiuretic hormone (ADH) and impaired water excretion. This occurs despite normal plasma volume, and results in dilute urine.

55. What is the appropriate thyroid hormone regimen for myxedema coma?

A. T4 (levothyroxine) is given at 1 mcg/kg of body weight IV over ten minutes, and then 150 mcg every day. T3 (liothyronine) is given at 20 to 35 mcg IV every 6 hours until symptoms improve.

B. T4 (levothyroxine) is given at 2 mcg/kg of body weight IV over five minutes, and then 100 mcg every day. T3 (liothyronine) is given at 10 to 25 mcg IV every 12 hours until symptoms improve.

C. T4 (levothyroxine) is given at 20 mcg/kg of body weight IV over 60 minutes, and then 200 mcg every day. T3 (liothyronine) is given at 100 to 250 mcg IV every 12 hours until symptoms improve.

D. T4 (levothyroxine) is given at 2 mg/kg of body weight IV over 15 minutes, and then 100 mg every day. T3 (liothyronine) is given at 10 to 25 mg IV every 24 hours until symptoms improve.

Answer: B. T4 (levothyroxine) is given at 2 mcg/kg of body weight IV over five minutes, and then 100 mcg every day. T3 (liothyronine) is given at 10 to 25 mcg IV every 12 hours until symptoms improve.

Explanation: The goals of treatment for the patient with myxedema coma include identifying the cause, correcting electrolyte and fluid imbalance, replacing hormones, and supportive care.

56. Jenna has been admitted to the ICU for diabetic ketoacidosis (DKA). Her insulin drip is currently at 6 units per hour, and she is receiving 0.9% NS at 75 cc/hr. Her blood sugar has decreased from 780 down to 270, and her anion gap is 25. The CCRN is ordered to check blood sugar every hour. At this point, what change in her care may the nurse expect?

A. No changes in therapy.

B. Discontinue the insulin drip, and decrease blood sugar checks to every four hours.

C. Change the intravenous fluid to D5NS and continue the insulin drip.

D. Change the intravenous fluid to 0.45% NS and continue the insulin drip.

Answer: C. Change the intravenous fluid to D5NS and continue the insulin drip.

Explanation: Once the blood glucose falls below 300 mg/dL, D5NS should be added to slow the drop in glucose. The hourly glucose checks will be continued, and the anion gap will be slowly lowered to less than 20.

57. Which type of hemophilia is a deficiency in clotting factor IX?
A. Hemophilia A
B. Hemophilia B
C. Hemophilia C
D. Hemophilia D

Answer: B. Hemophilia B

Explanation: Hemophilia is a disorder of clotting, and approximately 85 percent of people with this condition are men because these are X-linked recessive disorders. Hemophilia results in free bleeding or the propensity to bleed easily, but there are several levels of symptoms. Hemophilia A, also called classic hemophilia, is an abnormality or deficiency in clotting factor VIII. Hemophilia B is a deficiency in clotting factor IX. Hemophilia C mostly affects Ashkenazi Jews, and is a deficiency in clotting factor XI. There is no hemophilia D.

58. A five year-old female child has recently received immunizations. She is admitted to the ICU with bruising, petechiae, purpura, epistaxis, and retinal hemorrhages. What does this patient likely have?
A. Hemophilia A
B. Idiopathic thrombocytopenia purpura (ITP)
C. Disseminated intravascular coagulation (DIC)
D. None of the above

Answer: B. Idiopathic thrombocytopenia purpura (ITP)

Explanation: Idiopathic thrombocytopenic purpura (ITP) is an autoimmune condition where isolated thrombocytopenia occurs with normal bone marrow. With ITP, there is a decrease in the number of circulating platelets and an absence of toxic exposure to diseases that is associated with a low platelet count. In the U.S., ITP occurs in 7 out of 10,000 people, affecting females twice as more often than males. The signs and symptoms include recent immunization or a viral illness, petechiae, bruising, purpura, gingival bleeding, epistaxis, GI bleeding, and retinal hemorrhage.

59. Which type of heparin-induced thrombocytopenia (HIT) can be life-threatening and is an immune-mediated condition?
A. Type 1 HIT
B. Type 2 HIT
C. Type 3 HIT
D. Type 4 HIT

Answer: B. Type 2 HIT

Explanation: Heparin-induced thrombocytopenia (HIT) affects patients who are exposed to heparin. Type 1 HIT presents within the first two days of heparin therapy and is a non-immune disorder. Type 2 HIT is an immune-mediated condition that occurs four to nine days after heparin exposure. This condition can lead to life-threatening complications as well as loss of limbs.

60. When the first exposure to the allergen occurs, the body releases large amounts of:
A. Antihistamine
B. Neurotransmitters
C. Epinephrine
D. IgE antibodies

Answer: D. IgE antibodies

Explanation: When the first exposure to the allergen occurs, the body releases large amounts of IgE antibodies. However, with repeat exposures, this IgE will trigger histamine and other cytokines to be released. These chemicals cause serious systemic issues, such as bronchial constriction, pulmonary edema, hypovolemia, and shock.

61. **George was injured on the job, and has not been active since. He now has a deep vein thrombosis (DVT) and has been on a heparin drip for four days. Which would indicate that he is at a therapeutic level of heparin?**
A. His platelet count is 100,000.
B. His activated partial thromboplastin time is 43 seconds.
C. His Cullen's sign is negative.
D. Is IV insertion site is no longer oozing blood.

Answer: B. His activated partial thromboplastin time is 43 seconds.

Explanation: The activated partial thromboplastin time (aPTT) of 43 seconds is a therapeutic result, which is standardized at 2 to 2 ½ times the normal time for a patient's blood to clot, which is 20 to 30 seconds.

62. **How does low-molecular weight heparin (LMWH) differ from other heparin?**
A. LMWH is less stable than unfractionated heparin.
B. LMWH is more stable than unfractionated heparin.
C. LMWH is more difficult to administer than unfractionated heparin.
D. LMWH has more side effects than unfractionated heparin.

Answer: B. LMWH is more stable than unfractionated heparin.

Explanation: LMWH, such as Lovenox, is so stable that aPTTs are not required, and it is easily administered in the home setting.

63. **Patients on immunosuppressive medications must be protected with:**
A. Neutropenic precautions
B. Standard precautions
C. Droplet precautions
D. Air-borne precautions

Answer: A. Neutropenic precautions

Explanation: Immunosuppression is a deficit in the immunological system that causes a person to have an increased risk for infection. The CCRN should be aware that patients who are on medications that suppress the immune system must be protected with neutropenic precautions.

64. Chemical substances of the central nervous system that excite, inhibit, or alter the response of another cell are called:
A. Neuroglials
B. Neurons
C. Neurotransmitters
D. Dendrites

Answer: C. Neurotransmitters

Explanation: The entire nervous system is made up of two types of cells: neuroglial cells and neurons. Neurotransmitters are chemical substances of the central nervous system that excite, inhibit, or alter the response of another cell. Each neuron releases neurotransmitters in the nervous system. Dendrites are components of neurons that receive nerve signals.

65. The central nervous system (CNS) structure that controls voluntary movement and balance is the:
A. Cerebrum
B. Cerebellum
C. Hypothalamus
D. Brainstem

Answer: B. Cerebellum

Explanation: The CNS includes the brain and spinal cord. The cerebrum is a brain component that controls memory, thought, and senses. The cerebellum coordinates movement, balance, and fine motor ability. The brain stem controls breathing and consciousness. The diencephalon consists of the hypothalamus and thalamus.

66. **A patient is admitted to the ICU and has had a recent cerebral aneurysm with subarachnoid hemorrhage (SAH). What symptoms would the CCRN expect?**
A. Respiratory depression and constricted pupils
B. Back pain and auditory hallucinations
C. Delirium and confusion
D. Headache and altered level of consciousness

Answer: D. Headache and altered level of consciousness

Explanation: A cerebral aneurysm often leads to subarachnoid hemorrhage (SAH), which is a life-threatening condition. Signs and symptoms include headache, face pain, seizures, altered level of consciousness, autonomic disturbances, visual symptoms, respiratory distress, epistaxis, nuchal rigidity and dilated pupils.

67. **Jerry is a 17 year-old baseball player who was admitted to the ICU following a head injury that involved blunt force trauma to the left side of his head. The CCRN understands that which of the following is the most sensitive indicator of Jerry's status?**
A. Intracranial pressure (ICP) monitoring
B. Vital signs
C. Level of consciousness
D. Glasgow Coma Scale scores

Answer: C. Level of consciousness

Explanation: The patient's level of consciousness (LOC) is the most sensitive indicator of neurologic status. After a blunt head injury, the brain tissue is sensitive to small changes in glucose and oxygen levels, Also, if cerebral edema occurs, changes to glucose and oxygen occur, and this affects LOC.

68. **Sharon was a passenger in a motor vehicle accident, and she sustained a basilar skull fracture. Of the following signs, which differentiates the basilar fracture from one of the anterior fossa?**
A. Battle's sign
B. Epistaxis
C. Raccoon eyes
D. Retinal hemorrhage

Answer: A. Battle's sign

Explanation: Battle's sign is ecchymosis over the mastoid bone that appears 12 to 24 after the injury. Raccoon eyes, sub-conjunctival hemorrhage, and rhinorrhea are signs of an anterior fossa fracture.

69. **Of the following lab studies, which ones are used to diagnose multiple sclerosis (MS)?**
A. Electrolytes, glucose, and CBC
B. Cerebrospinal fluid evaluation, coagulation studies, and sedimentation rate
C. Syphilis testing, CBC, and drug screen
D. Fluorescent treponomal antibody absorption (FTA-ABS), cerebrospinal fluid evaluation, and sedimentation rate

Answer: D. Fluorescent treponomal antibody absorption (FTA-ABS), cerebrospinal fluid evaluation, and sedimentation rate

Explanation: For MS, a diagnostic cerebrospinal fluid evaluation includes colloid gold curve, slightly increased protein, and a negative syphilis (RPR). Also, the patient is asses with the FTA-ABS and sedimentation rate.

70. The three main criteria for diagnosis of brain death include all of the following EXCEPT:

A. Coma
B. Absence of brainstem reflexes
C. Absence of respirations
D. Apnea

Answer: C. Absence of respirations

Explanation: Brain death is the irreversible loss of brain functions. There are three main criteria for a diagnosis of brain death: coma, absence of brainstem reflexes, and apnea. The diagnosis of brain death is made by brain stem reflex assessment and a single apnea test.

71. Absence of electrical activity on an electroencephalogram (EEG) during ___ minutes or more of recording is indicative of brain death.

A. 15
B. 30
C. 45
D. 60

Answer: B. 30

Explanation: There are several diagnostic tests to confirm brain death, such as angiography (absence of intracerebral filling at the circle of Willis), MRI angiography, radionuclide angiography, nuclear brain scan (absence of uptake of isotope in the brain parenchyma or vasculature), transcranial Doppler US (small systolic peaks in early systole without diastolic flow, which indicate increased ICP), and EEG (absence of activity after 30 minutes).

72. Of the following, which is not a type of encephalopathy?
A. Alcoholic encephalopathy
B. Anoxic/hypoxic encephalopathy
C. Hypertensive encephalopathy
D. Neurogenic encephalopathy

Answer: D. Neurogenic encephalopathy

Explanation: Alcoholic encephalopathy occurs when a person drinks excessive alcohol repeatedly and it alters brain activity. Anoxic/hypoxic encephalopathy occurs when brain tissue is deprived of oxygen, leading to loss of overall brain function. Hypertensive encephalopathy occurs when blood pressure elevated and alters brain function, such as with a hypertensive crisis. Infectious encephalopathy occurs when patient has encephalitis, from bacteria, virus, or fungi, and it alters the brain tissue and/or the meninges. Ischemic encephalopathy occurs when small blood vessels that take blood to the brain narrow and there is generalized decreased flow of blood.

73. When a patient dies from status epilepticus, what is the mechanism of death?
A. Aspiration pneumonia
B. Head trauma from a fall during a seizure
C. Development of hypermetabolic state within the brain
D. Airway blockage, which leads to cerebral hypoxia

Answer: C. Development of hypermetabolic state within the brain

Explanation: With status epilepticus, the amount of glucose and oxygen in the brain is decreased, and this leads to the release of glutamate. Increased levels of glutamate causes an influx of calcium into the neurons, and this leads to cell injury and death.

74. All of the following are diagnostic findings for hydrocephalus EXCEPT:
A. Tense fontanel
B. Head circumference > 95th percentile for age
C. Dilated scalp veins
D. Increased ICP

Answer: B. Head circumference > 95th percentile for age

Explanation: Hydrocephalus is a disturbance of cerebrospinal fluid (CSF) formation, absorption, and/or flow, which causes an increase in CSF volume in the central nervous system (CNS). With this condition, head circumference > 98th percentile for age, and other findings include: dilated scalp veins, tense fontanel, increased intracranial pressure (setting-sun sign, retracted upper lids, and visible sclera above the iris), papilledema, unsteady gait, and increased reflexes.

75. The usual dose of thrombolytic therapy (rtPA) is:
A. 0.9 mg/kg for up to 90 mg, with 10 percent to the total dose given as a slow push bolus, and the other 90 percent given over one hour.
B. 0.5 mg/kg for up to 100 mg, with 30 percent to the total dose given as a slow push bolus, and the other 70 percent given over one hour.
C. 0.9 mg/kg for up to 80 mg, with 20 percent to the total dose given as a slow push bolus, and the other 80 percent given over one hour.
D. 0.5 mg/kg for up to 90 mg, with 20 percent to the total dose given as a slow push bolus, and the other 80 percent given over one hour.

Answer: A. 0.9 mg/kg for up to 10 mg, with 10 percent to the total dose given as a slow push bolus, and the other 90 percent given over one hour.

Explanation: Dose of rtPA is 0.9 mg/kg (maximum 90 mg). Ten percent of total dose is given as IV bolus, the rest as infusion over 60 minutes. rtPA is recommended within 3 hours of onset of ischemic stroke.

76. Following an intracranial hemorrhage, how is coagulopathy corrected?
A. Administer vitamin K
B. Give fresh frozen plasma
C. Use of protamine
D. All of the above

Answer: D. All of the above

Explanation: One of the treatments for intracranial hemorrhage is to correct coagulopathy. This involves the administration of vitamin K, fresh frozen plasma, protamine, and/or platelets.

77. With secondary intraventricular hemorrhage, where is the blood?
A. In the ventricles
B. In the parenchymal
C. In the subarachnoid areas
D. Any or all of the above

Answer: D. Any or all of the above

Explanation: Intraventricular hemorrhage (IVH) is the presence of blood in the ventricular system of the brain, which can lead to obstructive hydrocephalus. With primary IVH, the blood is in the ventricles, whereas with secondary IVH, the blood in in the parenchymal or subarachnoid areas, as well as the ventricles.

78. A 52 year-old white male with HIV is in the ICU. He is immunocompromised and recently had syphilis. He is currently being treated with antibiotics and antiviral agents. He now has confusion, drowsiness, seizures, and edema. What does this indicate?
A. A neurologic infection
B. A reaction to the antibiotics
C. A normal response to the antiviral medication
D. All of the above

Answer: A. A neurologic infection

Explanation: Encephalitis is inflammation of the brain, and meningitis is inflammation of the membranes that cover the brain and spinal cord. Neurologic infections lead to symptoms of confusion, drowsiness, seizures, and edema. They are often seen in patients who have compromised immune systems, such as someone with HIV/AIDS.

79. Of the following muscular dystrophy (MD) treatments, which one is given in order to slow the muscle degeneration process?
A. Antibiotics
B. Corticosteroids
C. Immunosuppressant drugs
D. Anticonvulsants

Answer: B. Corticosteroids

Explanation: MD is a group of 30 inherited diseases or more. These conditions cause loss of muscle and muscle weakness. Many forms of MD appear during infancy or childhood, whereas others do not appear until mid-life or later. Treatment involves: corticosteroids to slow muscle degeneration; immunosuppressant drugs to delay damage to muscle cells; anticonvulsants to prevent and control seizure activity; and antibiotics to treat respiratory infections.

80. What chronic, debilitating neuromuscular disorder results in tingling in the legs (initial symptom) followed by tingling of upper body and extremities, paralysis, absent reflexes, and protein in the cerebrospinal fluid (CSF)?
A. Myasthenia gravis (MG)
B. Muscular dystrophy (MD)
C. Guillain-Barré syndrome
D. Multiple sclerosis (MS)

Answer: C. Guillain-Barré syndrome

Explanation: Guillain-Barré syndrome causes the patient's immune system to attack his or her peripheral nervous system (PNS). Damage occurs to the nerves, and as a result, the patient's muscles have difficulty responding to the brain. The exact cause of this condition is unknown, but it may be triggered by surgery, infection, or a vaccination.

81. Robert is a 33 year-old man with a small brain tumor that is located at the skull base. What type of neurosurgery will he likely have?
A. Functional neurosurgery
B. Neuro-endoscopy
C. Craniotomy
D. Stereotactic neurosurgery

Answer: B. Neuro-endoscopy

Explanation: Functional neurosurgery is a special procedure used to manage epilepsy, movement disorders, and pain, and is typically done by placing and fixing a frame on the scalp to stabilize the frame into position and under local anesthesia. Neuro-endoscopy is a minimally invasive treatment for deep seated brain tumors and masses of the skull base. A small fiber optic lens is used to visualize the tumor(s) that lie(s) within the ventricular system of the brain, and biopsy is done during this procedure. A craniotomy is a procedure in which a skull bone flap is removed so the surgeon can reach the tumor. Stereotactic neurosurgery involves 3D imaging to locate and treat various targets of the nervous system.

82. Which seizure phase involves the actual seizure activity when the patient is unconscious and unresponsive?
A. Prodromal phase
B. Aural phase
C. Ictal phase
D. Post-ictal phase

Answer: C. Ictal phase

Explanation: With the first phase (the prodromal phase), there is activity and signs that occur before the seizure, such as headache and depressed mood. During the aural or second phase, there is a sensation that can be visual, auditory, visceral, or gustatory in nature (aura). The ictal phase involves the actual seizure activity when the patient is unconscious and unresponsive. The post-ictal phase occurs immediately after seizure activity, and during this stage, the patient will be disoriented, drowsy, confused, and have no memory of what happened.

83. Which seizures are characterized by brief and sudden arm muscle contractions, and do not cause unconsciousness?
A. Atypical absence seizures
B. Myoclonic seizures
C. Clonic seizures
D. Atonic seizures

Answer: B. Myoclonic seizures

Explanation: Absence seizures occur during childhood and often appear in clusters (dozens or hundreds of times per day), and they only last 5 to 10 seconds. Atypical absence seizures usually begin before the age of five years, are associated with mental retardation, last longer than absence seizures, and the patient will have muscle spasms. Myoclonic are characterized by brief and sudden arm muscle contractions, and the patient does not lose consciousness. Clonic seizures are characterized by rhythmic, repetitive movements of the face, neck, and arms, with movement being symmetric and bilateral. Tonic-clonic, also called grand mal, is the most common generalized seizure, and can lead to tongue biting, limb fractures, and head trauma; the patient will have violent shaking and muscle contractions. Atonic seizures involve sudden loss of muscle control, so the patient will often fall to the floor or out of the chair.

84. Following acute abdominal trauma, ecchymosis of the umbilicus is called:
A. Grey Turner sign
B. Cullen sign
C. Guarding
D. Rigidity

Answer: B. Cullen sign

Explanation: The signs and symptoms of acute abdominal trauma include ecchymosis of the flanks (Grey Turner sign), ecchymosis of the umbilicus (Cullen sign), abdominal pain, GI hemorrhage, hypovolemia, peritoneal irritation, abdominal bruit, guarding, rigidity, and/or rebound tenderness.

85. The family members of a patient with severe biliary obstruction and cirrhosis notices that their father has multiple excoriations and scratches over his skin. They express concern that the patient is being abused. What should the CCRN say?
A. "He probably got out of his restraints and fell."
B. "Because of the high bilirubin levels, he scratches his skin unconsciously."
C. "Because of the high glucagon levels, he scratches his skin unconsciously."
D. "He has ICU psychosis and is hitting at himself."

Answer: B. "Because of the high bilirubin levels, he scratches his skin unconsciously."

Explanation: The CCRN should acknowledge the family members' concerns and provide education. High bilirubin levels lead to deposits in the skin, which irritate the patient and lead to scratching. Also, with cirrhosis, PT, PTT, and INR levels are increased, which cause bleeding and hematomas to occur.

86. **Jacob is a 50 year-old Jewish man admitted to the ICU with unintentional weight loss (25 pounds), anorexia, fatigue, and chronic diarrhea with bloody mucus. Upon examination, his respiratory rate and heart rate are both elevated, and he is hyper-thermic. When the CCRN gets his laboratory results, she notices his hemoglobin is 6.8 g/dL, and his hematocrit is 20%. What is the likely condition?**
   A. Cholecystitis
   B. Pancreatitis
   C. Ulcerative colitis
   D. Diverticulitis

Answer: C. Ulcerative colitis

Explanation: UC is more common in Jewish males, and causes blood loss through the bowels, which leads to anemia and fatigue, as well as weight loss and anorexia. Cholecystitis usually does not cause diarrhea or blood loss through the bowels. Pancreatitis will cause more abdominal pain and rebound tenderness, without bloody, mucous-filled loose stool. Diverticulitis typically causes diarrhea, but not loss of blood and anemia.

87. **A complication of hepatic failure is hepatorenal syndrome, which is caused by:**
   A. Vasodilation
   B. Release of mediators
   C. Increased renal blood flow
   D. Increased circulating plasma

Answer: B. Release of mediators

Explanation: Hepatorenal syndrome is caused by release of mediators, which leads to vasoconstriction that diverts the flow of blood to the kidneys. When the patient develops ascites, circulating plasma decreases.

88. The CCRN is caring for a patient with an acute GI hemorrhage. All of the following are acceptable treatments for this condition EXCEPT:
A. Blood transfusions
B. IV fluid administration
C. Gastric lavage
D. High-dose IV beta blockers

Answer: D. High-dose IV beta blockers

Explanation: The patient with an acute GI bleed will be treated with blood transfusions, IV fluid administration, gastric lavage, surgical repair if necessary, and high-dose IV proton pump inhibitors (for patients with peptic ulcer).

89. A small bowel obstruction (SBO) is caused by postoperative adhesions in _____ of cases.
A. 40%
B. 50%
C. 60%
D. 70%

Answer: C. 60%

Explanation: A small bowel obstruction (SBO) is caused by postoperative adhesions in 60 percent of cases, with malignancy, hernias, and Crohn's disease causing the other 40 percent. SBO is characterized as either partial or complete and can be simple or strangulated.

90. Of the following, which is a medical emergency and requires laparoscopy?
A. Inflammatory bowel disease (IBD)
B. Malignant tumor
C. Intra-abdominal abscess
D. Strangulated obstruction

Answer: D. Strangulated obstruction

Explanation: Inflammatory bowel disease (IBD) is not an emergency, and is treated with high-dose steroids, bowel rest, and surgical treatment with bowel resection and/or strictureplasty. A malignant tumor requires surgical resection when feasible, and it is an urgent, not emergent, situation. An intra-abdominal abscess is treated by CT scan-guided drainage. A strangulated obstruction is a medical emergency and requires laparoscopy.

91. What procedure, used to treat gallstones and evaluate jaundice, is done with and endoscope inserted through the esophagus, stomach and the first portion of the small intestine, and when the scope reaches common bile duct, the physician injects dye and takes x-rays?
A. Endoscopic retrograde cholangiopancreatography (ERCP)
B. Endoscopic ultrasound (EUS)
C. Flexible sigmoidoscopy
D. Upper GI endoscopy

Answer: A. Endoscopic retrograde cholangiopancreatography (ERCP)

Explanation: ERCP is done with and endoscope inserted through the esophagus, stomach and the first portion of the small intestine. When the scope reaches common bile duct, the physician injects dye and takes x-rays. The ERCP is done to evaluate abdominal pain, gallstones, tumors, scar tissue, and jaundice.

92. One of the complications of cirrhosis that is treated by phlebotomy is:
A. Ascites
B. Portal hypertension
C. Hemochromatosis
D. Wilson disease

Answer: C. Hemochromatosis

Explanation: Cirrhosis is a diffuse hepatic process characterized by abnormal liver nodules and fibrosis. The majority of cases of cirrhosis are due to chronic alcohol consumption, but the progression of liver injury to cirrhosis can occur in just a few weeks. In the treatment of this condition, phlebotomy is used for hemochromatosis, prednisone and azathioprine for autoimmune hepatitis, interferon and antiviral agents for hepatitis of viral origin, Trientine and zinc for Wilson disease, and diuretics, paracentesis, and shuts for ascites.

93. In the patient with portal hypertension, how is portal pressure reduced?
A. Insertion of a shunt
B. With an anti-secretory agent by IV infusion
C. With a diuretic agent by IV slow push
D. NG tube placement

Answer: B. With an anti-secretory agent by IV infusion

Explanation: Portal hypertension is usually caused by cirrhosis. Two important factors that lead to the development of portal hypertension are vascular resistance and altered blood flow. Treatment involves NG tube placement, replacement of volume loss, administration of vasoconstrictors, control of esophageal varices bleeding, balloon tube tamponade, and transjugular intrahepatic portosystemic shunt (TIPS). Portal pressure reduction is done with an anti-secretory agent by IV infusion.

94. What body waste product contributes to hepatic encephalopathy?
A. Ammonia
B. Glucose
C. Urea
D. Bilirubin

Answer: A. Ammonia

Explanation: Hepatic coma, also called hepatic encephalopathy, is the loss of brain function related to the inability of the liver to remove blood toxins. Ammonia is produced by the body when proteins are digested and broken down, and if the liver cannot remove this substance, it accumulates in the bloodstream.

95. More than 70 percent of cases of acute pancreatitis are associated with:
A. Opiate abuse
B. Alcohol abuse
C. Tobacco abuse
D. Sedative abuse

Answer: B. Alcohol abuse

Explanation: Acute pancreatitis is inflammation of the pancreas that affects men more often than women. More than 70 percent of cases of acute pancreatitis are associated with alcohol abuse, but the condition is also linked to blockage of the pancreatic duct, trauma, and autoimmune conditions.

96. The inner portion of the kidney is called:
A. Cortex
B. Medullar
C. Hilum
D. Nephron

Answer: Medullar

Explanation: The kidneys control pH balance (acid/base), secrete berenin, vitamin D, and erythropoietin, and stimulate red blood cell production. The cortex, hilum and medullar are the outer, middle and inner portions of the kidney, respectively.

97. All of the following occurs in acute renal failure (ARF) EXCEPT:
A. The glomerular filtration rate (GFR) decreases.
B. The excretion of nitrogenous waste decreases.
C. Electrolytes become imbalanced.
D. Fluid levels are balanced.

Answer: D. Fluid levels are balanced.

Explanation: In ARF, the glomerular filtration rate (GFR) decreases, the excretion of nitrogenous waste is greatly reduced, and electrolyte and fluid balance cannot be maintained.

98. What type of renal failure occurs from damage to the renal tubular epithelium from nephrotoxins or injury?
A. Acute nephrotic syndrome
B. Acute tubular necrosis
C. Acute tubular sepsis
D. Acute renal hemorrhage

Answer: B. Acute tubular necrosis

Explanation: Acute tubular necrosis (ATN) is a condition that is considered intra-renal, with 75 percent of cases being of this type. The majority of hospital-acquired renal failure is ATN, which occurs from damage to the renal tubular epithelium from nephrotoxins or injury.

99. **Which diet would be most appropriate for the patient with chronic renal failure (CRF)?**
A. Low sodium, high protein
B. Low fat, no dairy, high protein
C. Low fat, low protein, low sodium
D. Regular diet

Answer: C. Low fat, low protein, low sodium

Explanation: Chronic renal failure (CRF), also known as chronic kidney disease (CKD) is the slow loss of renal function over time. The usually diet is low fat, low protein, and low sodium.

100. **All of the following patients are at risk for hypernatremia EXCEPT:**
A. An 82 year-old woman who has suffered an infection and had elevated temperatures.
B. A 78 year-old man who has underwent abdominal aneurysm repair surgery.
C. A 38 year-old woman who is on fluid restrictions due to renal insufficiency.
D. A 39 year-old man who is on ACE inhibitor therapy.

Answer: D. A 39 year-old man who is on ACE inhibitor therapy.

Explanation: Hypernatremia occurs when either too much water is lost or too much salt is ingested or received into the body. Older adults are at risk for hypernatremia following fever or surgery due to volume depletion and a diminished thirst mechanism. Also, patients on diuretic therapy or fluid restrictions are at risk for hypernatremia.

101. The CCRN is caring for a patient with renal disease who has recently experienced medication changes. The patient has peaked T waves and a prolonged PR interval on ECG. He now is complaining of abdominal cramping, fatigue, and muscle weakness. The CCRN notices that patient is somewhat lethargic. What is the likely cause of this?

A. Hyperkalemia

B. Hypokalemia

C. Hypernatremia

D. Hyponatremia

Answer: A. Hyperkalemia

Explanation: Elevated potassium in the blood stream will stimulate the release of aldosterone, which triggers retention of sodium. The most common cause of hyperkalemia is renal disease, acidosis, sodium depletion, aldosterone deficiency, and excessive intake of potassium supplements. The signs and symptoms of hyperkalemia include ECG changes (peaked T waves, prolonged PR interval, and wide QRS complex), muscle weakness, fatigue, lethargy, and abdominal cramping. If left untreated, cardiac arrest is likely.

102. Tracy, a 27 year-old secretary, is having lymphocytopheresis and plasma exchange for progressive MS. The anticoagulant used is citrate. After starting the procedure, she reports tingling. Which of the following series of lab results should the CCRN check?

A. PT with INR, potassium, sodium, and chloride

B. Ionized calcium, PT, PTT, and ABGs

C. ABGs, ACT, and ionized calcium level

D. Potassium sodium, and magnesium

Answer: C. ABGs, ACT, and ionized calcium level

Explanation: Citrate binds with calcium in the bloodstream and then metabolizes into sodium bicarbonate. Therefore, the sodium and phosphate alkaline levels go up. ABGs, ACT, and ionized calcium levels will show the extent of the citrate binding. The tingling sensation occurs due to a decrease in the amount of calcium in the body's tissues.

103. **A deficient supply of oxygen to the body that occurs from abnormal breathing and oxygen supply, which leads to generalized hypoxia, is:**
A. Asphyxia
B. Cyanosis
C. Epistaxis
D. Infarction

Answer: A. Asphyxia

Explanation: Asphyxia (asphyxiation) is a deficient supply of oxygen to the body that occurs from abnormal breathing and oxygen supply, which leads to generalized hypoxia. This affects the body's tissues and organs. Causes of asphyxia include obstruction or constriction of airways due to asthma or laryngospasm, blockage of the airway from a foreign body, or near-drowning.

104. **When a patient has sepsis, endotoxins stimulate the body to produce tumor necrosis factor (TNF). When this occurs, the TNF stimulates:**
A. Increased ICP
B. Increased retention of CO2
C. Production of parathyroid hormone
D. Platelet aggregation and neutrophil activation

Answer: D. Platelet aggregation and neutrophil activation

Explanation: TNF stimulates platelet aggregation, neutrophil activation, and also increases capillary permeability and the release of IL-1, IL-6, and IL-8.

105. All of the following are common causes of allergic reactions EXCEPT:
A. Bee stings
B. Latex
C. Shellfish
D. Wool

Answer: D. Wool

Explanation: Anaphylaxis is a type of allergic reaction that is life-threatening. It is caused by a reaction to a chemical or allergen. Once the patient is exposed, the immune system becomes sensitized to it, and anaphylaxis is likely. With anaphylaxis, the body tissues release histamine and other chemicals that cause the airways to restrict. Common causes of anaphylaxis include medications (antibiotics, NSAIDs, aspirin and some vitamins), environmental agents (pollen, mold, dust, or chemicals), foods (peanuts, shellfish, and eggs), latex (found in most medical supplies), and bites and stings (from wasps, bees, spiders, ants, and other insects).

106. This type of MODS occurs in a single organ, and other organs sequentially suffer failure or dysfunction:
A. Immediate
B. Delayed
C. Accumulation
D. Basic

Answer: B. Delayed

Explanation: Failure of multiple organs and systems is referred to as multi-organ dysfunction syndrome (MODS). This is caused by shock, hemorrhage, infection, burns, trauma, allergy, or severe acute pancreatitis. Immediate (primary) dysfunction occurs simultaneously in two or more organs and is due to a primary disease. Delayed (secondary) dysfunction occurs in a single organ, and other organs sequentially suffer failure or dysfunction. Accumulation dysfunction is caused by chronic disease.

107. **Gretchen is a 74 year-old Caucasian female admitted to the ICU. Here vital signs are: T 98.8, HR 148, RR 38, and BP 88/58. The CBC review shows a white count of 11,500. Gretchen reports that she was treated for a complicated kidney infection approximately three weeks ago. She has no abdominal pain, rigidity or guarding, and no flank pain is noted. What is the likely cause of her current health status?**
A. Appendicitis
B. Renal calculi
C. Systemic inflammatory response syndrome (SIRS)
D. Multi-organ dysfunction syndrome (MODS)

Answer: D. Multi-organ dysfunction syndrome (MODS)

Explanation: A renal calculi or appendicitis would lead to pain, and SIRS is usually associated with a WBC count of <4,000 or >12,000. MODS is a condition that results from a direct injury to an organ.

108. **Jeff is an alcoholic that was admitted to the ICU for complications associated with cirrhosis. Thiamine was added to his IV fluids because:**
A. Thiamine will decrease the symptoms of DTs.
B. Thiamine is a potent sedative, and patients who are withdrawing from alcohol often are anxious and combative.
C. Thiamine can prevent complications related to substance abuse.
D. Thiamine deficiency is common among alcoholics, and administering it will prevent damage to the brain from Wernicke's syndrome.

Answer: D. Thiamine deficiency is common among alcoholics, and administering it will prevent damage to the brain from Wernicke's syndrome.

Explanation: Wernicke's syndrome occurs from thiamine deficiency, which is common in people who abuse alcohol chronically.

109. All of the following are signs and symptoms of septic shock EXCEPT:
A. Tachycardia
B. Hypertension
C. Fever
D. Confusion

Answer: B. Hypertension

Explanation: Sepsis is the body's response to bacteremia or infection. Septic shock occurs when sepsis causes hypotension due to sepsis, not hypertension. Having certain diseases and conditions can put a patient at risk for sepsis, such as a weak immune system, heart valve abnormalities, and chemotherapy treatment.

110. Of the following, which is NOT a criterion for systemic inflammatory response syndrome (SIRS)?
A. Body temperature greater than 38°C(100.4°F) or less than 36°C(96.8°F)
B. Tachypnea greater than 20 breaths per minute
C. Arterial partial pressure of carbon dioxide less than 4.3 kPa (32 mmHg)
D. Heart rate lower than 60 beats per minute

Answer: D. Heart rate lower than 60 beats per minute

Explanation: SIRS is a serious condition related to organ dysfunction and failure. SIRS, like sepsis, is related to suspected or confirmed infection. This clinical condition can lead to respiratory distress syndrome, renal failure, central nervous system dysfunction, and/or gastrointestinal bleeding. The criteria for SIRS include:

- Body temperature greater than 38°C(100.4°F) or less than 36°C(96.8°F)
- Tachypnea greater than 20 breaths per minute
- Arterial partial pressure of carbon dioxide less than 4.3 kPa (32 mmHg)
- Heart rate greater than 90 beats per minute
- Leukocytes less than 4,000 cells/mm³ (4×10^9 cells/L) or greater than 12,000 cells/mm³ (12×10^9 cells/L) or the presence of more than 10% immature neutrophils (left shift)

111. The pH of a chemical substance determines if it is:
A. Acidic or alkaline
B. Toxic or nontoxic
C. Harmful or safe
D. Potent or dilute

Answer: A. Acidic or alkaline

Explanation: Caustics and corrosive substances can cause tissue injury, which occurs by accepting a proton (alkaline product) or donating a proton (acidic agent). The pH of a chemical substance determines if it is acidic or alkaline. To treat the patient, the CCRN must identify the specific substance ingested, the time and nature of the exposure, the duration of contact, and any treatment received.

112. Of the following signs and symptoms, which is NOT related to severe injury from ingestion of a caustic or corrosive substance?
A. Altered mental status
B. Viscous perforation
C. Stridor
D. Cough

Answer: D. Cough

Explanation: The signs and symptoms of severe injury include altered mental status, viscous perforation, stridor, hypotension, peritoneal signs, and shock.

113. The information material used when treating a patient who has ingested a poison is called the:
A. Material Service Diagnosis Sheet
B. Material Safety Data Sheet
C. Measurable Safety Diagnosis Schedule
D. Measurable Service Data Schedule

Answer: B. Material Safety Data Sheet

Explanation: Material Safety Data Sheets (MSDSs) have information related to the chemical or substance and instructions related to care.

114. Which type of alcohol ingestion and toxicity can cause renal failure and MODS, and occurs in three stages?
A. Isopropanol
B. Methanol
C. Ethylene
D. All of the above

Answer: C. Ethylene

Explanation: Ethylene glycol ingestion occurs in three stages:

- The neurologic stage (one hour after ingestion and last for up to 12 hours): Inebriation and hypocalcemia can cause muscle spasms and abnormal reflexes;
- The cardiopulmonary stage (12 to 24 hours after ingestion): The patient has hypertension, tachycardia, respiratory distress, and significant hypocalcemia.
- The renal stage (24 or more hours after ingestion): Symptoms of acute renal failure occur, and the patient can hyperventilate, suffer multiple organ dysfunction, and go into a coma.

115. Folinic acid at a dose of 1 mg/kg - and repeat in four hours - is given for which type of alcohol toxicity?

A. Methanol
B. Isopropanol
C. Ethylene
D. All of the above

Answer: A. Methanol

Explanation: Treatment for methanol toxicity includes folinic acid at a dose of 1 mg/kg and repeat in four hours.

116. Linda was admitted to the ICU due to confusion, bradycardia, seizures, and abdominal pain. The ER physician suspected opioid overdose and gave her naloxone. However, it had no discernible effect, and now, Linda is lethargic and suddenly develops hypotension. She admits to the CCRN that she is a "body packer." Appropriate treatment would be:

A. Activated charcoal, vasopressors, and sodium bicarbonate
B. Antiemetics, bronchodilators, and gastric lavage
C. Sodium bicarbonate and hemodialysis
D. Bowel irrigations, anticonvulsants, and intubation with mechanical ventilation

Answer: D. Bowel irrigations, anticonvulsants, and intubation with mechanical ventilation

Explanation: The term "body packer" means a person who transports drugs in one or more body cavities. This patient's packet has ruptured, causing her to have symptoms of opioid overdose. The treatment would involve irrigating the bowel, administering anticonvulsants, and using mechanical ventilation, as respiratory depression is likely.

117. For the patient with a pulmonary embolism, which of the following statements is true?
A. Metabolic alkalosis will develop.
B. Heparin is used to dissolve the clots.
C. Respiratory acidosis will occur.
D. Normal D-dimer results will rule out the pulmonary embolism.

Answer: D. Normal D-dimer results will rule out the pulmonary embolism.

Explanation: An elevated D-dimer level is often caused by a pulmonary embolism and other conditions. If this level is normal, PE is not likely. Hyperventilation occurs with PE and leads to hypoxemia and respiratory alkalosis, not respiratory acidosis or metabolic alkalosis. Also, heparin will not dissolve clots related to PE.

118. Which of the following patients is at risk for some type of abuse?
A. A 4 year-old child of a single mother.
B. A 22 year-old woman living with her boyfriend who drinks alcohol.
C. A 78 year-old woman who resides with her daughter in a subdivision.
D. A 16 year-old adolescent who is pregnant and lives alone.

Answer: B. A 22 year-old woman living with her boyfriends who drinks alcohol.

Explanation: There are several risk factors for abuse, including dementia, social isolation, shared living situations with an abuser, increased opportunity for contact, and exposure to perpetrators with such characteristics as drug and alcohol misuse, mental illness, and criminal history. Living with a single parent (choice A), being pregnant (choice D), and being elderly (choice C) are not risk factors.

119. What type of elder abuse involves lack of basic needs provision, such as hygiene, eyeglasses, dentures, preventive healthcare, and safety measures?
A. Physical
B. Emotional
C. Neglect
D. Abandonment

Answer: C. Neglect

Explanation: The National Center on Elder Abuse (NCEA) has identified seven categories of elder abuse. These are: physical, emotional/psychological, neglect, financial/material exploitation, self-neglect, and abandonment. Neglect is when the basic needs are not met of the patient, such as hygiene, safety concerns, food, clothing, and shelter.

120. All of the following are true concerning domestic abuse EXCEPT:
A. Approximately 1,000 victims seek treatment each year in the U.S. for domestic abuse.
B. It is not just one event; rather it is continuous pervasive or methodical use of these tactics by someone who wants control and power over the partner.
C. Studies have shown that the perpetrators of domestic violence were abused as children.
D. It also involves economic coercion that a person uses against his or her intimate partner.

Answer: A. Approximately 1,000 victims seek treatment each year in the U.S. for domestic abuse.

Explanation: According to the U.S. Department of Health and Human Services (DHS), as many as 1 million victims of domestic violence seek treatment each year in America. Around 900,000 children are identified to be victims of abuse and/or neglect each year. Research suggests that approximately 30 percent of families are affected by one or both of these problems.

121. Long-term consequences in children related to domestic abuse include all of the following EXCEPT:
A. Depression
B. Post-traumatic stress disorder (PTSD)
C. Obsessive compulsive disorder (OCD)
D. High tolerance to abuse and violence

Answer: C. Obsessive compulsive disorder (OCD)

Explanation: Experts have identified several negative effects that domestic violence has on children. There are three categories of childhood problems that are directly connected to domestic violence exposure: cognitive and attitude problems; behavioral, emotional, and social problems; and long-term consequences, such as depression, post-traumatic stress disorder, and a higher tolerance for abuse and violence.

122. What is a form of abuse or neglect where the parent or caregiver fabricates or causes a child's illness or injury, which subjects the child to unnecessary medical evaluation and treatment?
A. Munchausen syndrome
B. Munchausen syndrome by proxy
C. Munchausen syndrome by self
D. Morehouse syndrome

Answer: B. Munchausen syndrome by proxy

Explanation: Munchausen syndrome by proxy is a form of abuse or neglect where the parent or caregiver fabricates or causes a child's illness or injury, which subjects the child to unnecessary medical evaluation and treatment. This can often result in hospitalization, morbidity, or death. The mother is the usual person with Munchausen, and she is usually someone with medical knowledge. A typical pattern is seen in multiple visits to physicians, hospitals, and clinics.

123. A CCRN is taking care of a two year-old child in the ICU who suffered a fractured skull following a car accident. The nurse notices doughnut pattern burns on the child's body, but the diaper area is not affected. What could this indicate?
A. Trauma from the vehicle accident
B. Immersion burns
C. Bite marks
D. Chemical burns

Answer: B. Immersion burns

Explanation: Immersion burns have a doughnut pattern with the central area spared from wearing a diaper or a stocking line of demarcation where the child's foot was held in water.

124. Antisocial behavior is related to:
A. Aggression
B. Violence
C. Both A and B
D. Neither A nor B

Answer: C. Both A and B

Explanation: Antisocial behavior is related to violence and aggression. Violence is the result of aggression, whereas aggressive behavior is based on hostility and impulsion.

125. Of the following patients, which one exhibits signs of antisocial behavior?

A. A 78 year-old man who is confused and combative following surgery.
B. A 28 year-old man who has poor memory, difficulty concentrating, and reports that he hears a humming noise in his right ear.
C. A 30 year-old woman who is impulsive and seeks out compliments.
D. A 44 year-old woman who is depressed and anxious.

Answer: C. A 30 year-old woman who is impulsive and seeks out compliments.

Explanation: Antisocial behavior is any disruptive act or acts that causes hostility and aggression toward other persons. These behaviors occur along a severity continuum, which includes defiance of authority, total neglect for the rights of others, and repeated violations of social rules and the law. Antisocial people often lack empathy, have a need for admiration, are impulsive, and are excessively emotional. Delirium, dementia, depression, and anxiety are risk factors for antisocial behavior, however.

126. The patient with violence and/or aggressive tendencies should be referred to:

A. Social services
B. Psychiatric care
C. Community programs
D. All of the above

Answer: D. All of the above

Explanation: The patient with violence and/or aggressive tendencies should be referred to psychiatric care, social services, and community programs.

127. All of the following are risk factors for antisocial behavior EXCEPT:
A. Schizophrenia
B. Delirium
C. Dementia
D. Cerebral vascular accident

Answer: D. Cerebral vascular accident

Explanation: The risk factors for antisocial behavior include environmental stressors, genetic and neurobiological factors, history of violence, depression, schizophrenia, substance use/abuse, manic behavior, delirium, dementia, and unstable living situations.

128. What behavioral disorder involves a sudden change in cognition, such as disorientation, memory deficit, perceptual disturbance, and language disturbance?
A. Delirium
B. Dementia
C. Bipolar disorder
D. Generalized anxiety disorder

Answer: A. Delirium

Explanation: For a DSM-V diagnosis of delirium, the patient must have disturbances in attention, such as reduce ability to focus, sustain, and shift attention, loss of conscious awareness, change in cognition, such as disorientation, memory deficit, perceptual disturbance, and language disturbance, and evidence from history, physical examination, and/or laboratory tests that the delirium is caused by a medical condition, medication, intoxicating substance, or more than one of these things.

129. Approximately ___ percent of acute care hospital admission patients have delirium listed as one of the secondary diagnoses.
A. 5
B. 10
C. 15
D. 20

Answer: C. 15

Explanation: Approximately 15 percent of acute care hospital admission patients have delirium listed as one of the secondary diagnoses.

130. Treatment for delirium involves all of the following EXCEPT:
A. Fluid and nutrition
B. Reorientation techniques
C. A stimulating environment
D. Evaluation for Polypharmacy

Answer: C. A stimulating environment

Explanation: The appropriate environment for the patient with delirium is a quiet, well-lit, and relaxed atmosphere.

131. All of the following are known causes of dementia EXCEPT:
A. Stroke
B. Tumor
C. Brian injury
D. Carotid stenosis

Answer: D. Carotid stenosis

Explanation: Dementia is the loss of mental skills that affects the patient's daily life and activities of daily living. Dementia has a gradual onset and worsens over time. It is caused by damage or injury to the brain, or changes in the brain, such as tumors, strokes, or accidents. Alzheimer's disease is the most common cause of dementia.

132. **Sally M. is an 85 year-old patient admitted to the ICU following a cardiac episode. She has trouble with word usage, trouble recalling recent events and doesn't recognize her pastor or his wife when they visit. Her family members report that this has gradually been getting worse. What does Sally have?**
A. Delirium
B. Dementia
C. Bipolar disorder
D. Depression

Answer: B. Dementia

Explanation: Dementia has a gradual onset and worsens over time. The signs and symptoms of dementia include memory loss, trouble recalling recent events, difficulty recognizing places and people, trouble with word usage, problems planning and performing certain tasks, judgment errors, difficulty controlling emotions, depression, lack of hygiene, visual hallucination (seen in dementia with Lewy bodies), and personality changes and unusual behavior (seen in frontotemporal dementia).

133. **Of the following drugs to treat dementia, which one is used for hallucinations and agitation?**
A. Stimulant
B. Antidepressant
C. Cholinesterase inhibitor
D. Antipsychotic

Answer: D. Antipsychotics

Explanation: Antipsychotics are used in patients with hallucinations and agitation. Stimulants, such as methylphenidate, can help with the symptoms of dementia and depression. Antidepressants, like the SSRIs, are used to treat depression. Cholinesterase inhibitors stop the breakdown of acetylcholine (neurotransmitter), which increases the amount available in the brain to improve mental function.

134. This syndrome is one of the leading causes for mental retardation and is the result of a change in the FMR1 gene, where a small section of the gene code is repeated on a specific area of one of the chromosomes:

A. Down syndrome

B. Fragile X syndrome

C. Cerebral palsy

D. Autism

Answer: B. Fragile X syndrome

Explanation: Fragile X syndrome is one of the leading causes for mental retardation. This condition is the result of a change in the FMR1 gene, where a small section of the gene code is repeated on a specific "fragile" area of the X chromosome. This disorder affects males more often than females, and the patient presents with hyperactive behavior, a large forehead, a prominent jaw, lack of eye contact, and mental retardation.

135. What developmental condition occurs when there is damage to the motor control centers of the brain in utero, during childbirth, or after birth?

A. Autism

B. Fragile X syndrome

C. Down syndrome

D. Cerebral palsy

Answer: D. Cerebral palsy

Explanation: Cerebral palsy (CP) is a group of non-progressive conditions that lead to physical and mental disabilities, and it occurs when there is damage to the motor control centers of the brain in utero, during childbirth, or after birth. Patients with CP have motor disturbances, as well as problems with sensation, cognition, perception, behavior, and communication.

136. **A patient with a severe form of autism spectrum disorder (ASD) will exhibit any or all of the following EXCEPT:**

A. Inability to communicate with others

B. Avoidance of eye contact

C. Fixation on certain objects

D. Lack of pain sensation

Answer: D. Lack of pain sensation

Explanation: Autism spectrum disorder (ASD) is a blanket term used to describe a complicated developmental delay that usually presents during the first three years of life. Autism affects the child ability to communicate and interact with other people. Adult patients with ASD often have a lack of language or limited communication skills, avoidance of eye contact, repetitive behaviors, and fixation on certain objects.

137. **Janice is a 38 year-old female diagnosed with multiple sclerosis (MS). She has reported lack of interest in usual things, excessive sleeping, and hopelessness. The CCRN recognizes these signs as what condition that is associated with MS?**

A. Dementia

B. Delirium

C. Depression

D. Dysthymic disorder

Answer: C. Depression

Explanation: Many neurological conditions cause depression, including Alzheimer's disease, cerebrovascular accident, multiple sclerosis, and brain tumors.

138. **Elise is a 24 year-old Caucasian female admitted to the ICU for endocarditis. She currently also complains of insomnia, fatigue, trouble focusing, relationship problems, and irritability. She is not sleeping, has erratic speech, appears to be excessively energetic, and has racing thoughts. Additionally, her mother reports she was "totally different" two weeks ago, and at that time, she slept a lot, had excessive sadness, and expressed hopelessness and suicidal ideation. What should the CCRN suspect?**

A. Dysthymic disorder

B. Bipolar disorder

C. Depression

D. Delirium

Answer: B. Bipolar disorder

Explanation: Bipolar disorder is characterized by periods of mania (highs) followed by episodes of depression (lows). A patient is diagnosed with bipolar disorder when he or she has cyclic episodes of highs and lows for more than two weeks. A patient with bipolar disorder will complain of insomnia, fatigue, trouble focusing, relationship problems, and irritability. In the depressive state, the patient may sleep a lot, have excessive sadness, and express hopelessness and suicidal ideation. Manic patients do not sleep, and they usually have excessive energy, erratic speech and racing thoughts.

139. **Of the following, which is NOT associated with generalized anxiety disorder (GAD)?**

A. Substance abuse

B. Substance withdrawal

C. Depression

D. Delirium

Answer: D. Delirium

Explanation: Generalized anxiety disorder (GAD) is a pattern of repetitive or constant worry and anxiety. Substance abuse, substance withdrawal, and depression are all associated with anxiety.

140. Alcohol withdrawal involves "the shakes," which are tremors experienced 12 to 24 hours after the patient's last drink. These tremors are related to:
A. Over-excitation of the CNS
B. Over-excitation of the PNS
C. Low thiamine levels
D. High ammonia levels

Answer: A. Over-excitation of the CNS

Explanation: Alcohol withdrawal involves "the shakes," which are tremors experienced 12 to 24 hours after the patient's last drink. These tremors are related to over-excitation of the CNS and are accompanied by diaphoresis, tachycardia, insomnia, and anorexia.

141. Andrew is a 16 year-old homeless teen who was admitted to the ICU for pulmonary edema and endocarditis. He has multiple skin abscesses and areas of cellulitis on his arms and legs. The recent lab results show that he has tested positive for hepatitis C. What is the likely cause of his problems?
A. Alcohol dependence
B. Opiate dependence
C. Marijuana dependence
D. Hallucinogen dependence

Answer: B. Opiate dependence

Explanation: Heroin is the most commonly abused opiate along with prescription oxycodone, morphine, methadone, hydrocodone, fentanyl, and codeine. Chronic users develop conditions such as cellulitis, skin abscesses, mycotic aneurysms, pulmonary edema, endocarditis, HIV, and various forms of hepatitis.

142. Elijah is a 22 year-old college student who was admitted to the ICU for hemodynamic instability. He reports that he has been "partying" with his friends for the last three days. He is experiencing paranoia, tachycardia, anorexia, insomnia, agitation, elevated blood pressure, tachypnea, and diaphoresis. What is the likely cause of his condition?

A. Opiate withdrawal
B. Alcohol withdrawal
C. Acute cocaine intoxication
D. Acute hallucinogen intoxication

Answer: C. Acute cocaine intoxication

Explanation: Cocaine can be inhaled, snorted, smoked, injected, or used topically. Acute intoxication leads to paranoia, tachycardia, anorexia, insomnia, agitation, elevated blood pressure, tachypnea, and diaphoresis. Withdrawal from cocaine and amphetamines is fairly mild, with symptoms of headache, increased appetite, and depression.

143. Which of the following tools is used to assess patient's use and consumption of alcohol and/or substances?

A. The Stanford-Binet questionnaire
B. The CAGE questionnaire
C. The Mini Mental Status Evaluation (MMSE)
D. The GAGE questionnaire

Answer: B. The CAGE questionnaire

Explanation: Most healthcare workers use the CAGE questionnaire when assessing substance use/abuse. This includes:

- Cutting down – Has anyone ever asked you to cut down on drinking/use?
- Annoyed – Have people annoyed you by criticizing your drinking/use?
- Guilt – Do you feel guilty about your drinking/use?
- Eye opener – Have you ever had to use or drink first thing in the morning to get rid of withdrawal symptoms?

144. Of the following, which is NOT a risk factor for suicide?

A. Age between 14 and 22 years
B. Strong family history of suicide
C. Drug use/abuse
D. Major life loss, such as death of a loved one or loss of job

Answer: A. Age between 14 and 22 years

Explanation: Risk factors for suicide include: definite plan for suicide, engaging in activities that indicate they are leaving life, strong family history of suicide, presence of a gun or weapon, psychotic symptoms, drug use/abuse, life loss (death of a loved one, loss of job, etc.), major depression, anxiety, or other mood disorder, experiencing hallucinations, and recent discharge from mental health facility.

145. CCRNs are accountable for functioning according to many guidelines, rules, and policies. Which of the following is NOT a directive that the nurse should follow?

A. Institutional policies
B. State Nurse Practice Act
C. ANA Standards of Practice
D. Nursing professor's instructions

Answer: D. Nursing professor's instructions

Explanation: Institutional policies, State Practice Acts, and the ANA's Standards are all policies and guidelines the professional nurse must follow. Instructions from a nursing professor do not hold a nurse legally accountable and are not directives for nursing practice.

146. An 82 year-old patient with a terminal condition has written a living will. In this document, she specifies that no heroic measures or aggressive actions be implanted to sustain her life or prolong her suffering. This is an example of her right to:

A. Advocacy
B. Autonomy
C. Privacy
D. Stability

Answer: B. Autonomy

Explanation: Autonomy is the ethical principle related to self-direction. A living will is an advanced directive that gives the patient the ability to maintain autonomy over decision making when she becomes incapacitated.

147. The CCRN identifies and assists with ethical and clinical concerns within and outside of the clinical environment and he or she is often the voice for those who cannot represent themselves, such as patients and family members. What is this role?

A. Moral agent
B. Ethical servant
C. Advocacy assistant
D. Clinical director

Answer: A. Moral agent

Explanation: Advocacy and moral agency involve working on another's behalf and representing the patient and family's concerns. The CCRN serves as a moral agent to identify and assist with ethical and clinical concerns within and outside of the clinical environment. Nurses are often the voice for those who cannot represent themselves, such as patients and family members.

148. **The American Association of Critical-Care Nurses (AACN) developed the Synergy Model of Patient Care in the 1990s to describe nursing practice based on eight key patient characteristics and eight nurse competencies. Of the following, which is NOT one of the model's assumptions?**
A. Patients are biological, social, psychological, and spiritual entities who are at a particular developmental stage in life.
B. The essential patient characteristics are associated with each other and cannot be viewed in isolation.
C. The essential patient characteristics are associated with each other and cannot be viewed in isolation.
D. The goal of nursing is to get the patient at an acceptable level of wellness, and death must never be an option.

Answer: D. The goal of nursing is to get the patient at an acceptable level of wellness, and death must never be an option.

Explanation: Choices A, B, and C are all assumptions of the Synergy Model. However, the goal of nursing is to get the patient at his or her optimal level of wellness, and death must be an acceptable outcome when it is inevitable.

149. **What is the idea that telling the truth is important when communicating with patients, family members, and other healthcare workers, especially in regard to medical diagnosis and treatments?**
A. Confidentiality
B. Justice
C. Beneficence
D. Veracity

Answer: D.

Explanation: While confidentiality, justice, and beneficence are all terms used for other ethical principles, veracity involves telling the truth, and is important when communicating with patients, family members, and other healthcare workers, especially in regard to medical diagnosis and treatments.

150. Which of the following concepts involves working patients, families, and healthcare providers to promote each person's contribution toward achieving realistic patient and family goals, and also encompasses multidisciplinary work with other healthcare professionals, community service members, patients, and families?

A. Collaboration

B. Beneficence

C. Veracity

D. Advocacy

Answer: A. Collaboration

Explanation: Collaboration involves working with patients, families, and healthcare providers to promote each person's contribution toward achieving realistic patient and family goals. This process encompasses multidisciplinary work with other healthcare professionals, community service members, patients, and families. The care environment should be one that is focuses on the best interest of the patient.

37969244R00184

Made in the USA
Lexington, KY
18 December 2014